"Boys, we've run outta time! Get your guns ready!"

With that, Abrams pointed the chopper right at the tracers coming up out of the jungle. Romanski, Robbie, and Wobbe all got a look of terror on their faces as it dawned on them all what Abrams was about to do!

The lead Army gunship was coming down, getting ready to unload a bunch of rockets right on the SEAL Team. They thought they were all VC. Abrams, coming in fast and low, pulled back on the stick and raised the collective, making his bird climb out to about 200 feet. He flared and came to a stop in a hover, effectively blocking the charging Army gunships from the SEALs on the ground. However, doing that put him right over Charlie's position. Talk about hanging your ass out to dry!

The shit didn't just hit the fan; the whole damn manure factory fell on it. No one even bothered to say they were receiving fire. That would have been redundant. Wobbe, Robbie, and Romanski had all the M-60s going without even letting up on the triggers. They could hear loud banging sounds as hundreds of rounds tore through their helicopter's skin. . . .

By Daniel E. Kelly:

SEAWOLVES: FIRST CHOICE

U.S. NAVY SEAWOLVES

The Elite HAL-3 Helicopter Squadron in Vietnam

Daniel E. Kelly

BALLANTINE BOOKS • NEW YORK

A Ballantine Book
Published by The Ballantine Publishing Group
Copyright © 2002 by Belle R. Kelly

www.ballantinebooks.com

ISBN 0-345-45510-X

Manufactured in the United States of America

First Edition: October 2002

OPM 10 9 8 7 6 5 4 3 2 1

Foreword

The story you are about to read is basically true. Due to the difficulty in tracking down the many people involved in this adventure, I had to take creative license in making the tale complete. I apologize in advance to those brave men who should have their correct names in this book. You know who you are, therefore I dedicate this work to you.

Some of the names and stories are completely accurate, and some have been created from bits and pieces of stories I have gathered from countless interviews. It would be almost impossible to write it in such a way as to distinguish one person or story from another, because so many run together, but it is possible to acknowledge particular groups and individuals who contributed to this book.

I give special thanks to the assistance of the Vietnam-era SEAL Team One personnel I spoke with at the year 2000 reunion in Buena Vista, Colorado. I also owe a lot to SEAL Team One member Frank Sparks. Without his friendship and ongoing help, I never could have put any of this together. Another SEAL Team One member who contributed to this work was Lou Hyatt. He has been a great friend and supporter.

Seawolf Detachment One members Fred "Buddy"

FOREWORD

Record, Lyle Nimmo, Mike O'Boyle, Steve McAllister, Lieutenant Bagley, and Commander Harker have also been invaluable to me.

I am also very grateful to Captain Robert W. Spencer. He unselfishly spent a great deal of his valuable time making a tape that he sent me from his home in Florida. Without his story, this book would never have taken shape. What's more, I consider him a great person, one whom there's no way I could ever thank for the commitment he made to the success of the first and only U.S. Navy Attack Helicopter Squadron of its kind. He is a true American hero whom I, for one, will never forget.

One more person that helped out was John Luscher. Again, this book could not have been made without his help. He was with Detachment Two during the 1968 Tet Offensive and is a plank owner, an original member, of HAL-3.

There are three more people that I need to thank. Writing a book like this places you on an emotional roller coaster. Whenever I was down, my two children, Derek and Jennifer, were always there to pick me back up. And then there's my lovely wife, Belle, the last person, but really the first, whom I must acknowledge. Belle has stood by me through the bad and the good for over thirty years.

Introduction

Both my books, *Seawolves: First Choice* and *U.S. Navy Seawolves,* came about due to the encouragement of SEAL Team Two plank owner Jim "Patches" Watson. We met at my first Seawolf reunion in Pensacola, Florida. He approached me about writing a book explaining to the world who we were. He said, "Pegleg, everyone knows about the SEAL Teams now, but no one has ever heard of you guys and you don't even exist anymore. That's not fair. If it hadn't been for the Seawolves, most of us SEALs wouldn't have made it back. You were some crazy sons of bitches, and the world should hear your story."

"Patches" put me in touch with the correct people to get my first book published. After that it was just a matter of getting the work done. I was able to finish *Seawolves: First Choice* and get all the stories backed up. That book is completely accurate.

U.S. Navy Seawolves is about why we were needed—the creation and existence of a United States Navy Helicopter Attack outfit. This was a first in naval aviation history. Not only that, but it consisted of personnel who had been put through a training program that had never been done before. Admiral

INTRODUCTION

Zumwalt and Commander Robert W. Spencer created this program with the assistance of the U.S. Army, Marine Corps, and Navy SEALs.

The U.S. Navy Helicopter Squadron HC-1 were the forerunners of this organization. I salute you as true pioneers. You put your lives on the line with minimal training, and a lot of disorganization, because the River Patrol Boats and SEALs needed you at once! Those brave men led the way in Southeast Asia until the Seawolves could be created. They were also instrumental in the final phase of the Seawolves' commissioning.

Movies were made by the Department of the Navy of HC-1 in action over in Vietnam. They were intended for use as a recruiting tool for sailors in boot camp who might want to volunteer. The whole operation was on a volunteer basis.

HAL-3, Helicopter Attack Light Squadron Three, the Seawolves, is the only unit in naval history that was commissioned and decommissioned outside of the United States. Another first.

Several thousand maintenance people with HAL-3 over a five-year period kept our seven detachments flying, and in the last days, two additional detachments. The two hundred men in the Seawolf combat teams never could have amassed the record-breaking statistics that they did without the incredible skill and courage of those guys in the hangars where the aircraft were prepped and repaired. They worked under the worst possible conditions, fixing all the damage we consistently put on our helicopters. Their devotion to duty saved a lot of lives. Those men have a definite place in the following record set by the first Navy Attack Helicopter Squadron.

INTRODUCTION

78,000 combat missions flown
131,000 flight hours
8,200 enemy killed
8,700 enemy vessels destroyed
9,500 enemy structures destroyed
17,339 decorations or medals awarded

The latter figure doesn't include all the medals that should have been awarded in the early days but weren't due to neglect of paperwork or because men were too busy flying combat missions—and flying the missions that never received approval from Saigon and thus couldn't be logged.

I draw to your attention my first book as well as this one. Gunner Lyle Nimmo was never awarded an Air Medal or anything else for that matter. He saved my life. Nothing is stated on his DD-214 that shows he did anything. I know of many more who never received recognition of any kind. That is something that needs to be rectified. I hope that this book somehow helps those unknown warriors.

Read on and learn of heroism that's never been told before.

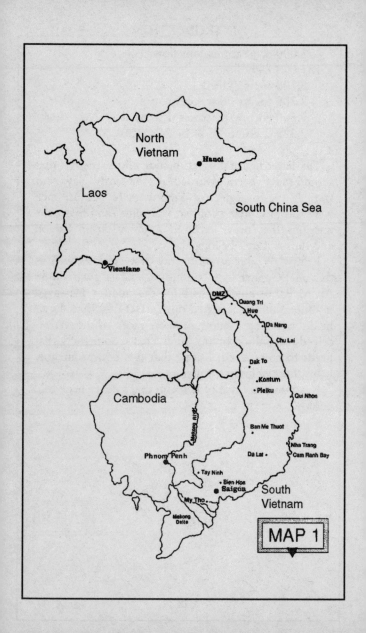

North
Vietnam

Hanoi

Laos

South China Sea

Vientiane

DMZ

Quang Tri
Hue

Da Nang

Chu Lai

Dak To

Kontum

Pleiku

Qui Nhon

Cambodia

Ban Me Thuot

Nha Trang

Phnom Penh

Da Lat

Cam Ranh Bay

Tay Ninh

Bien Hoa
Saigon

South
Vietnam

My Tho

Mekong
Delta

MAP 1

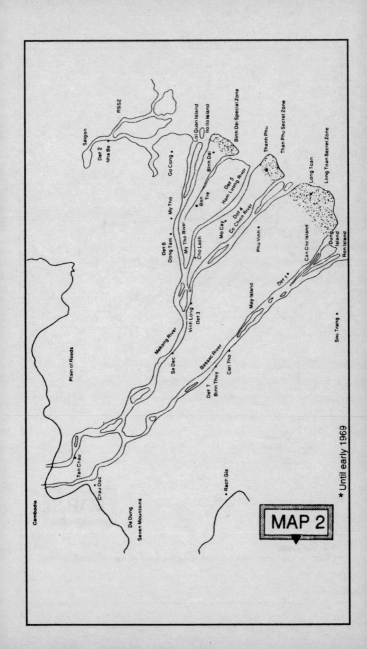

MAP 2

Cambodia

Plain of Reeds

Da Dung
Seven Mountains

Tan Chau
Chau Doc

* Rach Gia

Mekong River

Sa Dec

Vinh Long
Der 3

Bassac River

Binh Thuy
Der 7
Can Tho

Saigon
Der 2
Nha Be

RSSZ

Go Cong

Loi Quan Island
Ho Ioi Island

Binh Dai Special Zone

My Tho

Der 6
Dong Tam

My Tho River

Cho Lach

Binh
Dai

Ben
Tre

Der 5

Ham Luong River

Mo Cay

Der 4

Co. Chien River

Thanh Phu

Than Phu Secret Zone

Long Toan

Long Toan Secret Zone

Phu Vinh

May Island

Der 1*

Can Cho Island

Dung
Island
Ron Island

Soc Trang

* Until early 1969

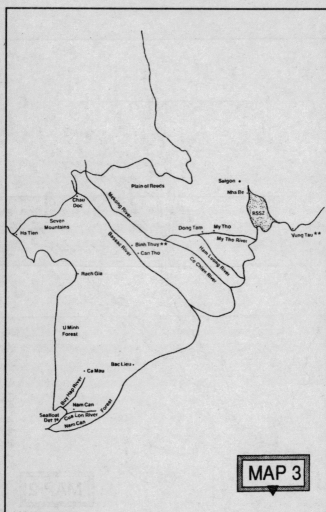

Plain of Reeds

Saigon •

Nha Be •

Chau Doc

Mekong River

Seven Mountains

• Ha Tien

Bassac River

Dong Tam • My Tho
                *
                My Tho River

• Binh Thuy **
• Can Tho

RSS2

Vung Tau **

Ham Luong River

Co Chien River

• Rach Gia

U Minh Forest

Bac Lieu •

• Ca Mau

Bay Hap River

Nam Can

Forest

Seafloat Det 1*

Cua Lon River

Nam Can

MAP 3

* After early 1969
** Vung Tau was Seawolf Mainbase until spring 1969, when it was moved to Binh Thuy.

U.S. NAVY
SEAWOLVES

1

Monsoon season. The night is covered with a blanket of humid air you could cut with a knife. It is perfectly still. The only evidence of movement is a lone, olive drab, thirty-one-foot-long fiberglass patrol boat drifting in the river. On board is a U.S. Navy SEAL Team frozen in time, sweat trickling down camouflaged faces with watchful eyes. Seven men wait silently around the twin .50s—two .50 caliber machine guns—on the front of the PBR (Patrol Boat, River) manned by one of the River Rat sailors. Another River Rat is at a single .50 caliber gun at the rear of the vessel. They watch for any sign that their position has been detected.

There's an old chief petty officer at the wheel, using all his experience to guide the PBR with its two diesel engines and jet pumps to its destination without making a sound. By nursing the throttles ever so gently and using the current, he navigates the river to get the SEAL Team where it wants to go. You can't hear the motors at idle speed because of the foam built around them to kill the noise.

Total darkness. With the thick cloud cover brought on by the approaching monsoon, you can't tell where the river stops and the jungle starts. That's where the fourth River Rat comes in. He's got his sweat-dripping face pushed into a large black rubber cup that has a radar screen inside it. It's the only way he can see the shoreline. A slight breeze begins to blow across the bow, signaling that the rain will start at any moment.

By whispering directions and using a combination of hand signals to the chief, the two of them maneuver the PBR in to the muddy bottom of the shallow water, which is the bank, as careful as a mother handling a newborn babe.

As the boat drifts to a complete stop on the bank, the SEALs slither over the side without making a sound, like a school of water snakes eager to get back home. As the last one leaves the PBR, the entire squad disappears from sight of the River Rats. They have been swallowed up once again by South Vietnam's insect-infested mangrove swamp in the Delta region.

Tom Moloney, the point man, is the first one to penetrate the dark jungle edge after leaving the muddy bank. A twenty-eight-year-old first class petty officer from Tennessee, the five-foot-nine Moloney is wearing tiger-striped fatigues and an olive drab rag, which used to be a T-shirt, stretched over the top of his head and tied in the back like a pirate's. Camo paint covers his face.

Moloney moves slowly, almost on his hands and knees in the mud, looking and feeling for booby traps. You don't move in a hurry in this swamp, doing what he's doing, unless you want to get sent home in a bag.

He carries a Stoner (a belt-fed M-16), with a 100-round drum of .223 ammo attached underneath, as with an old-fashioned tommy gun. He also has 800 rounds of belted ammo strapped around him, adding to the pirate image. Six V-40 grenades (each about the size of a golf ball), one concussion grenade, one gas grenade, two pop flares, and a directional flashlight with colored lens hang from his web gear. His first aid supplies consist of a waist pack with a can of serum albumin, two morphine syrettes, and battle dressing. Attached to his upper chest on his web gear is a Gerber Mk-1 knife with a Smith & Wesson model 22 and silencer in a shoulder holster. Last but not least, a LAAW rocket is strapped to his back.

Following in Moloney's tracks is twenty-two-year-old Fritz Heitjan. He carries an M-60 machine gun and enough ammo to bring a water buffalo to its knees. His face is painted light green, dark green, and black, like a confused zebra. A K-bar knife is taped to his shoulder, along with a directional flashlight with colored lens.

The third man to break the edge of the swamp is their leader, twenty-five-year-old lieutenant junior grade Richard Benedict from Wisconsin. At six feet two inches and 185 pounds, he projects a commanding presence. His weapon of choice is a CAR-15 (a stumpy-looking M-16). There are six magazines of ammo mounted on his web gear across the front of his chest, plus three more taped together in his gun, and on his back hangs a Starlight Scope.

Kane Kennedy, the radioman, is next in line. He's twenty-six years old, out of Georgia, five-ten and 160 pounds of dynamite. Kennedy's got a PRC-25 radio strapped to his back, with a computer card that keeps people from listening in. It scrambles the signal somehow. His weapon of choice is an M-203 (an M-16 with an M-79 grenade launcher mounted under the barrel).

Next is Richard Oliver, the twenty-five-year-old

corpsman. Along with the medical gear and copper sulfate, he carries an M-60 belt-fed machine gun with 400 rounds and the weight that comes with it. He's burly, at six-one and 195 pounds, and ready to kill as well as save.

Third class petty officer Vernon Barker comes right behind. The twenty-one-year-old has a Stoner in hand and a LAAW rocket strapped to his back, as well as a silenced Smith & Wesson under his arm, a K-bar knife on his shoulder, numerous grenades, and a first aid pouch with a canteen of water.

Twenty-two-year-old Texan Mo Marvin brings up the rear. He carries an M-60 and the responsibility of ensuring that Charlie doesn't sneak up on them from behind. Like Vernon, Mo is black, and at six-three and 215 pounds, even bigger than the Louisianan.

It's another body snatch mission, and the men look the part, in tiger stripes, camo green faces, and loaded down with enough killing tools for World War Three. The LT, Benedict, takes it as his responsibility to bring everyone back home alive. He's studied martial arts since he was a kid, put in four years at the Naval Academy, and has a degree in engineering. Yet here he is, getting eaten alive by unknown kinds of bugs in a faraway land, hunting and killing under the worst possible conditions, and for poverty wages. God, he loves it!

A slight breeze starts to blow through the jungle on this hot, humid night. There's no moon out, which is as it should be—the darker, the better.

The men are moving through the mangroves at a snail's pace, at times on their hands and knees. There's about four or five inches of water with mud underneath and a tangled mess of mangrove roots twisting and winding through, on top, and under the water, which makes it easy to trip and fall. And this is one place no one wants to fall. It contains everything from pungy sticks to trip wires with 81mm mortar shells attached to them. That'll ruin your day!

Benedict can see Heitjan out in front of him, moving along with his eyes fixed on Moloney in front of him and at the same time watching for movement to his right. Benedict is scanning to the left in sync with his CAR-15. Kennedy, the radioman, just behind him, is focused on his right, and so on, back to Mo, the rear guard, who's covering 180 degrees behind.

As they keep moving forward, it seems a contest to see who can be the quietest. You get extra points for being the first to see something in your assigned area. It's like trying to sneak up on a deer with your bow and arrow back home. Now, that takes some talent—just trying to see the deer before he sees you. And this jungle is thick.

Benedict's feet inside his boots are already soaked with the swamp water that's worked its way down and around his socks. The rest of him is a sweaty mess, with his tiger stripe fatigues sticking to his body. He thinks: Boy, is it hot.

The mosquitoes are terrible. He's already got welts coming up on his face and hands where he's been bit, and the mission's just getting started.

Wow! Look out! Heitjan just squatted way down, holding up one clenched fist. Moloney had heard or seen something ahead. Benedict signals too, so Kennedy and the rest will stop as well. All of them become part of the jungle, not a single muscle moving.

After what seems an eternity, but is just a couple of seconds, they find out what the deal was. There's something in the jungle moving rapidly toward them. It sounds like a bunch of people running their way. A cool breeze blows ahead of it. Then a curtain of water moves straight through the jungle, sweeping over the squad and on toward the river behind.

It's a monsoon storm, and as it approaches, it makes an eerie sound, bouncing off all the leaves in the jungle, working its way down through the three levels of canopy above. These rains, when they come, are like a wall of water walking across the Delta. Not much wind, just rain coming straight down. And in contrast and relief to the heat, it's wonderfully refreshing.

It is unnerving, though, since it can't be seen approaching. All you can hear is movement, from all that water hitting the jungle undergrowth.

As the cool rain makes its way through Benedict's hair and over his bandanna, then continues on down his back, he can feel his body being recharged with the comfort of the liquid overtaking the sticky, hot, sweaty feeling of cloth stuck to him everywhere.

The team slowly moves forward again, toward its objective. They all hope that the rain lasts. It makes them even harder to detect. Of course, it makes it harder for them to see as well.

Benedict doesn't like the men moving through the dense undergrowth so close together, but they have to be able to communicate. Occasionally, he swings his Starlight Scope around from his shoulder and glances through it to scan the surrounding area. With the rain, and it being so dark, it's harder to see through the scope. It looks like a green TV screen with a lot of snow. All he can make out are silhouettes of his men and the jungle background.

They keep edging forward through the mangroves as if balancing on a tightrope over the Grand Canyon, with their lives depending on every planted foot. Which of course they do! At this rate it will take them about two hours to travel one klick from the river to the village, where they'll find the man they're after.

He's a province chief. The intelligence gathered by the Provincial Interrogation Command, MACV (Military Assistance Command Vietnam), and COMNAV-FORV (Command Naval Forces Vietnam) says he's a major bad guy. There are pictures of him and how many guards he'll be traveling with, right down to the hooch where he'll be found within the village.

A flyover by Army chopper the day before will help locate the specific hooch. It will make the job much easier. Plus, the men spotted the perfect extraction point about two klicks north of the village, which had been the scene of a B-52 strike leveling that part of the jungle. The Army helicopter could come in and pick them up there.

The report went on to say that now was the time to grab the province chief because of the updated knowledge he had.

Shit! Benedict stops short. There goes Heitjan again! He dissolves down into the slush they're maneuvering through, his arm raised, his fist clinched, signaling that there's a problem. Moloney has stumbled onto something.

Between a combination of hand signals and lip reading, the message is passed back through the squad. Moloney came up on a trip wire. It's probably attached to an 81mm mortar round somewhere close by. The point man will mark the spot and then move on, stepping gingerly over the wire like a cat avoiding water. The mark is usually a twig or a leaf of some kind. After Heitjan goes over it, it's Benedict's turn, and he discovers that the mark is a stripped-off piece of bark.

Never, never be in a hurry! The LT knows this. If nothing else, he's going to come out of this with the patience of Job.

When he's over it, it's Kennedy's turn. Benedict points out the piece of bark that marks the spot, as Heitjan did for him. The LT wants to watch him but can't. He has to keep his focus on his job, which is the left side of the jungle and any movement that might signal an ambush. He knows the drill: never assume anything and be ready for everything!

Glancing back, he can tell that his radioman has made his move past the danger spot.

Next is Oliver. Benedict can't see him in all the rain and darkness, but as Kennedy continues moving forward, the LT knows that all is well with the rest of the squad behind.

Moving along at their slow, consistent pace, Benedict can feel his fingers on the CAR-15 getting that prunelike feeling from being wet so long. Like back home in his swimming pool, which he would just about live in during summer vacation. His toes in his boots are getting that same feeling. Water running down past his bandanna, across his forehead, and into and around his eyes makes him blink constantly. An eyelash every once in a while gets flushed into his eye. He hates it when that happens.

He knows you have to keep your focus and ignore

the little things in life. An eyelash in the eye won't kill you, but an AK-47 round will definitely change the expression on your face.

The rain is steady, just like the dark, as they keep moving like a snake winding through its own backyard, slowly and cautiously looking for that next meal. Nobody's in a hurry. They're all just concentrating on consistency in exact movements, and they focus on the job at hand.

As Benedict's feet, carefully, one at a time, slide through the four or five inches of water and down into the mud beneath, he feels the mangrove roots twisting and winding across the swamp, seemingly trying everything they can to trip him up. Finding that trip wire means there's going to be more ahead, and in this shit they're literally climbing through, it's going to be hard finding other traps. One thing about this job, it sure makes you stretch.

About thirty minutes later the rain starts to let up a little. Just in time for the baseball fanatic to alert them again. Way to go, Mr. Baseball! Keep up the good work! Benedict thinks. Another trip wire.

After marking it, he moves on. The rest of the men follow suit, taking their turns levitating over the stretched-tight fishing line blocking their path. Moloney must have some Indian in him somewhere, Benedict muses. He doesn't know how he seems to find these things in all this mess, but he's sure glad he does.

About the time they've all cleared the last trap, the rain picks up again. This time they aren't surprised by the incoming second storm as it makes the usual noise approaching and moves over the squad. They also have another inconvenience introduced to them that they're used to, though they still hate it: red biting ants washed out of the surrounding trees and down the backs and arms of their shirts.

Focus, motherfucker! Benedict tells himself. Ignore those little bastards and keep moving! Shit, he hates this. When this is all over and he's back home, he tells himself, he's going to kill every bug he can find. He hates bugs!

Oops! What's this? A different sign from the point man passes to Heitjan and on to Benedict, who thinks: I gotcha, bud! There's a pungy pit just off to their left. It looks to be about thirty feet long and about four feet wide, from the sticks that Moloney uses to mark it with.

As Benedict moves up to the spot and past, he can tell it's a deep pit, by how far down the sticks go that were cut off from the surrounding growth to mark the spot. All underwater. This could have been real nasty.

It shouldn't be much farther now. It's been almost two hours since they left the boat.

There ya go! Right on cue! Heitjan signals that they've arrived.

As they all freeze momentarily, Benedict pulls up the Starlight Scope to check out the area.

Through the static-green snowy picture, he can make out several hooches on stilts standing just one or two feet out of the water. Two raised lookout platforms are on either side of the closest grass hut to them, also about a foot out of the water. From their intel, the closest hut with the lookouts on either side is the location of the target. There's a figure of a man on top of each platform sitting like a Mexican on a siesta, plus one on the little front porch of the target hooch, who also appears to be asleep.

But Benedict bets they're not. It's just the rain that's

got them in that position. That's three security guards, which again is consistent with their info. So far, so good.

There are only a few feet between them, the guards, and the house they have to hit. That's how close they have to get to see, because it's darker than dark and the rain is still falling.

Smooth, quiet motion is the order of the day. Be invisible, becoming one with the jungle and water. With Stoner at the ready, Moloney has already started to make his move toward the lookout platform on the left, in accordance with the plan. Heitjan is moving to the right with his M-60. Kennedy moves up and out to Benedict's left with his M-203. Oliver moves up to his right with his M-60. Vernon and Mo split to the left and right, falling in between Moloney and Kennedy on one side and Heitjan and Oliver on the other, covering 180 degrees behind them.

They're all in place now in a half-moon formation covering forward and back, ready to collapse into a circle on the targeted hut. It's just about time for Moloney and Heitjan to do their thing.

Oh, shit! Geese! They're better than any watchdog could possibly be, and can they make a racket! Benedict pulls his Smith & Wesson model 22 with silencer from his shoulder holster and opens up on a goose that just rounded the neighbor's house. Vernon, not yet completely in his rearguard position after moving up, has noticed the watchdogs as well. Pulling his silenced S&W at the same time, he drops two geese that come out the front door of the same hut. So much for the watchdogs. Those silenced S&Ws were just that! You couldn't hear a sound, with all the rain coming down splashing on the swamped ground and jungle.

Without missing a beat, Moloney lets his Stoner hang freely around his neck, pulls the Gerber Mk-1 from its sheath, grabs his guard and shoves the knife into the side of the VC's head, behind and under the ear, scrambling his victim's brain and killing him instantly.

Heitjan, across the way, has come up behind his guard. He lets his M-60 hang loose around his neck. Pulling his K-bar out of the sheath on his web gear, he buries the knife up to the scabbard in the back of the guard's neck and into the base of the brain, dropping his victim like a wet rag.

Benedict moves his sights to the guard at the door of the targeted hut and squeezes off two rounds from his silenced gun into the VC's head. The man slumps over into a terminal nap.

Damn, that was fast! I love it! the LT thinks. He knows that this kind of teamwork only happens after you've been working together for a while. You get to know what everybody's going to do instinctively. The geese could have caused a serious cluster fuck.

Collapsing on the hooch, everyone sets up a perimeter around the house, covering the surrounding village and jungle. With rain still pounding out its tune on the swamp, Kennedy and Benedict hit the door, with Oliver as backup. The man they've come for is asleep on the floor all by himself. Nobody else there. It makes it easier. Pulling on his red-lensed flashlight, Benedict confirms that this is the guy. Kennedy ties his hands in front with plastic quick ties while the LT ties a gag over his mouth.

He is packed for traveling faster than a cowboy could tie up a cow in a rodeo. When he wakes up to the men tying him up, his eyes get so big he looks like a sumo wrestler at an all-you-can-eat buffet.

Outside, Moloney, Heitjan, Vernon, and Mo are in ankle-deep water, covering all four corners facing out away from the hooch, guns at the ready, just waiting for any surprises. They get the prisoner on his feet and move to the door.

2

To this point they haven't been compromised. So, because of the weather conditions, they can make for the LZ and their pickup by the quickest possible route. That's straight through the middle of the village and out the other side.

To make the trip through the jungle even faster, they won't blindfold the prisoner. Keeping him out in front, he can see where they're headed, which will motivate him to discover booby traps.

Benedict on his right and Kennedy on his left yank and drag him by the arms, with his hands tied in front, past the other huts and into the jungle on the far side. The rest of the squad is tagging and leapfrogging behind to cover the extraction. They know they don't have much time left before the scheduled pickup at the landing zone. The Army chopper is supposed to meet them at sunup at the bombed-out crater about two klicks away.

The rain still coming down, they move into the jungle's edge with their prize. Vernon, Mo, Oliver, Heitjan, and Moloney are close behind. They climb in and around the mangrove roots, fight the mud and water, and try not to trip. Kennedy and Benedict watch their compasses to make sure they're headed in the right direction. They're also pulling and tugging on the prisoner to scare him into keeping his eyes open so he can keep them from hitting any more traps. It makes for a challenging early morning stroll. On the bright side, the squad is definitely going faster than it did coming in.

They know that if their navigation is correct, they'll continue in this direction for about half a klick, then make a ninety-degree turn to the left and continue on for another one and a half klicks. That would punch them out into the open at the LZ, where the chopper should be waiting.

Benedict has his CAR-15 in one hand and an iron grip on the prisoner's arm with his other hand as they forge through the muck and mire of the South Vietnam jungle. Rain still pours down through the various levels of foliage above them, and the LT can feel the soreness in his leg muscles throbbing.

He keeps telling himself to just move and drag this guy who's going to tell them what they need to know to save more mothers back in the "World"—which is what the Americans in Vietnam called the U.S.—from getting that feared telegram delivered by the two uniformed officers who always come knocking. That thought seems to give Benedict the second wind he's looking for. Meanwhile, checking his compass, he's aware of where they are.

Time to make the left-hand turn, boys!

Changing directions, they begin the final leg of their trip. All Benedict can think of now is the seat in that chopper calling to him and the others. It won't be long now.

Glancing back, he can see Oliver right on their heels, doing his thing. He can't see beyond that because of the still-dark jungle they're moving through.

Slowly and steadily, they move forward, their feet sliding cautiously into the water, roots, and muck, watchful for anything that signals danger. A movement or twitch from the prisoner will tell them there's a trap ahead. All senses peaked, Benedict occasionally stops to check the Starlight Scope for anything it might reveal. And they're looking at their compasses, to double-check directions. Benedict scans right as Kennedy scans left, ready for anything at any moment that might explode into a shit storm. It seems to Benedict that he can feel every muscle strand in his body, as if his brain were taking inventory to make sure everything's functioning properly. The ant bites he got earlier, along with everything else, like sore muscles, can't be felt anymore, because his brain is too busy handling the more important stuff.

Keep looking, he tells himself. Keep scanning the darkness. Keep moving the feet forward, as fast yet as carefully as possible. Keep hold of that arm and watch the prisoner's reactions. Keep hold of the CAR-15, ready to cut loose with a shower of .223 machine-gun fire. Keep an eye on the compass to make sure you're still going in the correct direction. Keep those ears on active listening mode, hearing the rain and the slapping jungle growth and separating that from other sounds that shouldn't be there.

Two klicks in this stuff under these conditions is like walking ten miles, he thinks. Come on, LZ. You're out there somewhere close. I can just smell ya.

It hits him that they haven't found any booby traps

yet. That figures. He thinks: When you've got a free pass, like we do with this guy, you don't need it!

The overcast sky with the rain still falling starts showing a little light here and there. There's not much, though, because of the canopy of jungle over them. But there's just enough to know that the sun is about to introduce itself to the rain-soaked Delta. They can actually see each other now. That means they have to spread out a little farther.

Wow! We've arrived! It reminds Benedict of coming out of a movie theater back home, going from dark to light all of a sudden. Where are my sunglasses? he wonders.

In fact, it isn't that bright, but when you've been trying to see in darkness for so long and you come out of it, it's like pulling back the curtain in a dark room. The clearing is spread before them, the trees flattened by the B-52 strike earlier, the jungle wiped clean. They stop at the edge of the clearing and peer out into the light, not letting anyone get a chance at seeing them.

The sun's come up, all right. It's completely daylight. The dense cloud cover has light and dark patches in it. A typical monsoon sky.

Another thing Benedict notices: no Army chopper. *They should already be here, waiting for us!* Well, he knows all about what "should be" in life. That's usually not what happens.

Instinctively, the team spreads out and sets up a perimeter. They're back-to-back, ready for anything. The rain is really coming down now. Benedict scans the edge of the LZ, looking for any sign of movement. They're all squatted down with guns at the ready. Heitjan moves his red smoke grenade around in front of him in case they have to mark their position for the chopper once it gets there.

The water is running down the front of Benedict's camouflaged face as he sits there wondering where the chopper is. He doesn't even hear it flying around above them. Are they at the correct spot? Did they misnavigate?

He double-checks everything. *No! Damn it! We're at the right spot!*

He knows they can't wait there long. Charlie will be on their ass at any moment. If he doesn't hear chopper sounds soon, he knows they'll have to go to Plan B.

He hates the waiting! Things are starting to get too tense.

Looking at his watch, he thinks, Just a few more minutes. How many more, though? *Damn those Army pukes! Where the fuck are they?*

They can't wait any longer. There's only one thing to do: they have to break radio silence. The LT doesn't want to do it, but there's no choice. He motions to Kennedy to grab the prisoner while he uses the radio on Kennedy's back. Kennedy isn't about to let the prisoner get away and puts him in an uncomfortable hold around his neck with his knee in the middle of his spine. Ouch! It looks like it smarts, but he won't be going anywhere, and he sure won't make a sound either.

Benedict puts the radio/telephone to his ear and mouth. Trying to ignore the water washing one of his eyelashes into his eye again, along with some of the camo makeup, not to mention the ants biting the shit out of him, he keys the mike.

"Scorpion One to Bravo Six. Scorpion One to Bravo Six. Over."

Silence on the airwaves, followed by more silence. What's with this shit, anyway? he wonders.

"Scorpion One to Bravo Six. Scorpion One to Bravo Six. Over."

Still nothing!

Then he hears a familiar voice come back over the radio. "Scorpion One, Scorpion One. Scorpion Two. Over."

It's Chief Davis! The crazy old sea dog from the other half of the platoon. What's he doing on the radio? Benedict wonders. And then, suddenly, he knows. The Army chopper isn't coming.

"Scorpion Two. Scorpion One. Go ahead."

"Scorpion One. Scorpion Two. Bravo Six is a bust. Suggest Plan B. Over."

Well, fuck me!

"Scorpion Two. Scorpion One. We copy. Are you ready? Over."

"Scorpion One. Scorpion Two. We be hot to rock! Over."

"Jesus Christ, I sure hope so!" Benedict whispers under his breath as he hangs up the radio on Kennedy's back.

He pauses, then tells the squad, "Saddle up, boys! We're headed straight for the river!"

And not a minute too soon.

Crack, crack, crack, whiz!

They've all heard that familiar sound before—AK-47 fire, straight at their heads. But at least it's coming from behind them instead of from the direction they need to go.

Kennedy and Benedict break into a gallop around the edge of the clearing and head straight for the river as fast as they can stay upright with the cargo they're now dragging behind them. Mo, Vernon, Oliver, Heitjan, and Moloney are covering them, tearing up the jungle behind them in the direction of the enemy gunfire.

As they move, several AK-47s cut loose on full automatic. They're answered by M-16s, M-60s, M-79 grenades, and one LAAW rocket. One thing Benedict always liked about their little group: they were heavily armed mothers!

They plunge through the jungle, Kennedy and Benedict dragging the prisoner, the five guys close behind them leapfrogging away from the AK fire. Between their M-60s cutting loose, with an occasional burst of Stoner and a frag grenade tossed, topped off with a LAAW rocket chaser, it seems they're slowing down the advancing Viet Cong, of which they have no idea how many there are. All they know is that they have to get the prisoner to the boats in the river before those behind them catch up.

Careful where you put those feet, Benedict, the LT reminds himself. And: go quicker, be faster and more careful, faster, faster. Get through this alive, damn it. Where's that fucking river? Where was that fucking Army chopper? Can't think about that now! Got to keep my mind on what we're doing. Ain't got time to get mad! Just think and move. Think and move. Don't worry about the teammates behind. They're doing their job, you do yours. Get the prisoner to the boats in the river. Where's the river? Straight ahead now. Keep moving. Keep moving. Watch where you're putting your feet. How's Kennedy doing? He's okay. He's doing his job. You just keep doing yours.

Jesus Christ, if this bastard falls down one more time, I'm going to cut his throat right here! But he knows he can't kill him. Damn it all. He picks him up and keeps moving.

It seems he's running the 800 meters back at the Naval Academy four times over without stopping, and his coach is yelling at him to go faster all the way.

The rain stops abruptly, as if someone turned the valve off on the sprinkler system back home. Steam follows close behind. Sweat starts running off Benedict as fast as the rain was running off before. He wishes it would start raining again.

Then come the bugs. It seems the entire mosquito population of the world decides to have a family reunion on every square inch of his exposed flesh at once. He doesn't know which is worse—bugs, sore muscles, or getting shot. *What am I thinking?* he asks himself. Getting shot is the big winner there!

The AK fire is getting closer. He can hear his guys shooting more and more. The barrels have got to be getting hot as hell. According to his count, they're out of LAAW rockets. It's just grenades and guns now.

The big jungle leaves they keep running through would cut at them like razors if not for the long sleeves on their camos. It feels like he's jogging through a flooded cornfield back home. It sounds silly, he thinks, but paper cuts suck.

Where in hell is the river? Jesus, he wishes they had some helicopter gunships right now. That would be a godsend. Mail-order some 2.75 rockets right up Charlie's ass!

This little bastard is getting heavy. He sure better be worth it!

He can feel the blast of an M-60 firing right behind him. It's Heitjan. *Holy shit!* There's the river. And thank you, Jesus, there's the PBRs.

Four of them all together, gunning their engines, head straight into the bank.

It's always good to have an alternate plan. This location had been picked the day before just in case something like this happened. The Army was famous for leaving them with their butts hanging out to dry.

Benedict and Kennedy proceed with their prisoner out of the jungle and onto a mud bank that stretches into the water about four feet. They sink up to their knees in mud as the lead boat's bow slides right up to their chests. There are rope ladders draped over the front so they can pull themselves up out of the mud and drag the captured VC on board.

Kennedy goes up and over the top of the boat first. Then he drags the prisoner in, and Benedict follows. The suction of the mud is incredible, but it's nothing they haven't done many times before.

As Benedict makes it up and over the side into the boat, he turns and starts to secure their prize. He can hear the gunfire behind them getting closer. An occasional AK round zips out of the jungle and past his head.

Kyle Anderson, a twenty-one-year-old third class petty officer, is about six feet of country boy. Dressed in all his SEAL team gear, ready for war, he holds his Stoner in one hand and grabs the prisoner by the scruff of his shirt with the other. He lifts him clean off the deck, the prisoner's feet dangling in the air, manhandles him around and down below to secure him for the trip to the interrogation room at Nha Be.

Benedict turns again to see how his team is doing. They've just emerged from the jungle's edge, all present and accounted for and shooting like hell back into the swamp.

That's all he needs to know. He yells at the River Rats, "Give 'em hell, boys!"

The PBR's .50 caliber machine guns open up on the enemy fire as the rest of the SEAL platoon helps retrieve the five worn-out killers from the mud bank and pulls them onboard the four boats, meanwhile giving cover fire. Once the men are secure in their places, they all cut loose at the same time with their individual weapons. Twelve .50 caliber machine guns, eleven M-60s, five Stoners, three M-203s, and Benedict's CAR-15, all on full automatic. Like a giant weed eater, they cut a path through the jungle you could drive a truck through. Oh boy! Come on, Charlie!

As the boats back off the bank and turn upriver, they all keep firing at the jungle. To their surprise, three B-40 rockets come whizzing out at them, but they explode harmlessly on the other side of the river. One of them actually goes clear through the boat behind Benedict without exploding or hitting anyone. You haven't lived until you've had a B-40 rocket fly by your head, he thinks. It makes you feel like an eighty-five-year-old rooster in a barnyard of a thousand hens. Very lucky!

The gunfire from both sides slowly drifts away as they gain speed going farther upriver. Benedict takes inventory on his team and finds that everyone has come out without a scratch. Of course, that doesn't count the bug bites, assorted cuts and bruises, and numerous strained muscles. It brings back memories of the good old football days when he used to come in from practice, blood running down his legs and arms from hitting on the field, and his mom just about passed out from the sight. He just never noticed it. He thought it was part of the fun.

Now Benedict sits back on the fiberglass floor of this heaven-sent converted man-killer ski boat and waits for the endorphins to wear off. His face in the wind is comforted with the water spray coming up over the side of the boat, gently massaging it as they cut through the brown river water. You know what's great about these boats? he thinks. When you're cruising along, there are no bugs!

Chief Davis comes over and sits down next to him. Benedict turns to him and says, "Thanks, Chief! That was a close one! We were lucky!"

"No shit!" the chief says. "I had a feeling this might happen."

This wasn't the first time the Army had let them down. It seems they just didn't fly in bad weather or at night. Well, they did sometimes, but not all the time.

"Hey, Chief," Benedict says, "lets get with that Army pilot, Pete Eldridge—the one we've worked with before—and find out what the deal is. He's never let us down."

"Good idea, boss. I'll set it up as soon as we get back."

3
___

South Vietnam during monsoon season. After the rain stops, the sweltering heat moves in and does its thing on the muddy streets of the city. It turns them to dried reddish-brown dust in a matter of minutes. The air is so thick with humidity, you find it hard to breathe at times.

The hustle and bustle of downtown Saigon is its usual traffic hazard. Motor scooters, motorized three-wheeler rickshaws, and little taxis everywhere try to dodge the hundreds of bicycles and pedestrians up and down the streets moving here and there, doing their shopping. Little kids running back and forth doing who knows what. All sizes and shapes of Oriental people with their pajama-looking outfits or floor length dresses that would have passed as nightgowns back in the States. Everyone topped off with coolie hats except the young men and boys. They have combinations of stolen Army fatigues and American jeans and shirts they get on the black market.

Adding to the confusion are all the soldiers trying to make their way through the city crowd. Horns blowing, bicycle bells ringing, Army trucks, jeeps with machine guns mounted in back, South Vietnamese police vehicles, Australian, American, Korean, you name it.

Just about everyone in the free world is represented here in this exploding city of commerce, in this exotic paradise that has seen war for hundreds of years.

A generation of Vietnamese have no understanding of peace and know only two major businesses: growing and marketing rice, and . . . well, let's just call it entertaining the male species. Of course, there's another business that's never talked about: drugs. The black market is big business. It's always behind the scenes somewhere. It's hard to say which is bigger, the marijuana business or the heroin business. Poppy fields are all over this part of the world.

Just off the main street, among the many bars that cater to GIs, is a place called Frenchie's. It's staffed with gorgeous girls, the result of when the French were in Vietnam years before us. The girls are half round-eye and half slant-eye. Beautiful exotic bedroom eyes, flowing long black hair, long legs, and bodies to die for. It's the Nha Be SEAL Team and River Rats' favorite hangout in Saigon; it's their turf. It's where they always gravitate to, because of the heat—to get into the shade and grab hold of a cold beer as soon as possible.

This particular place has refrigerated American beer. How they got it or the refrigeration facilities is a mystery.

The men grab the ass or tits of the nearest barmaid and buy her a Saigon tea. (A famous drink the visiting GI is required to purchase in order for the barmaid to allow him to play with her tits or ass. If you play without purchasing the required drink, management will get pissed, and that's not good foreign relations.)

The drinking establishment is located in a three-story building made of concrete and wood. It used to be a hotel, but now it's a club, with the family of the owners living upstairs, plus extra sleeping quarters for those *other* guests. And believe me, it's a big family!

They live pretty well too. Color TV, standing floor fans, and they even have electric lights, but don't use them during the daytime. So the only light you get is what comes in through the windows and doors. Since there's only one door in front and only one window next to it, which has wooden shutters, there isn't much light.

The club or bar is located just inside the front door, in what used to be the lobby of the former hotel. There's enough space for twelve tables with chairs, and a long bar that goes down the right side of the room as you enter. There are eight bar stools lined up in front of the bar. Two standing floor fans, one in each of the back corners, really take the heat off. There's a large radio behind the bar that's tuned to some Vietnamese station playing their kind of music.

An Army pilot comes nonchalantly drifting in through the open door to the bar. He pauses at the entrance and removes a pair of flier sunglasses from his face to let his eyes adjust to the darkness inside. Standing tall in his Army fatigues, supporting silver pilot wings on his chest and captain bars on his collars, he stares into the dimly lit space he's about to invade. He can make out eleven guys sitting around three tables, all wearing olive drab fatigues with no markings as to rank, name, or occupation. The eleven vary between five feet eleven inches and six-foot-five, except for one, who's about five-foot-six. They all look good, like Olympic athletes look good. They have an air about them like "Are you sure you want to come in here and join us?"

Eight of the eleven men have girls sitting in their laps, all with big smiles on their faces. Three tables over, two River Rats are indulging themselves in a little foreign relations of their own. Each has a girl with him as well, but they're doing more feeling of the breasts and other things than drinking beer. The party has definitely begun.

An older Oriental man stands behind the bar cleaning glasses and doing what old bartenders do. At the far end of the bar there are two other girls. One sits on a bar stool, and the other is standing next to her, talking in Vietnamese.

The Army pilot moves toward the occupied tables, confidence and steadfastness in his gait. There's an empty chair at one of the tables. He goes straight for it.

"Hey, Pete, how the fuck are ya?" Richard Benedict bellows out to him.

"Still trying to keep you Navy pukes from getting your asses blown off!" he barks back as the two of them slap a hearty handshake. Then the flier sits down.

This is the famed Army pilot Pete Eldridge, whom everyone has heard so much about. He flies a Huey helicopter gunship in the Delta, and he's pulled Chief Davis and Benedict out of more than one hot spot during his many tours of Southeast Asia. The others have worked with him before but never gotten a chance to meet him.

"You know the chief!" Benedict says. "Let me introduce you to the others."

He goes around the tables doing the introductions. Chris Holland and Rock are sitting with him and the chief. Doc Stinehour, Brad Mitchell, and Kyle Anderson are at the adjacent table. Eric Red, Mikey Collier, Dan Lewis, and Shawn Roten are at the next table over. That makes up the remainder of the SEAL platoon. Richard Oliver, Mo Marvin, Vernon Barker, Tom Moloney, Fritz Heitjan, and Kane Kennedy are crashed back at the team hooch at Nha Be.

After all the introductions are done, Eldridge sits back to relax. Before he has a chance to say anything, his nostrils are filled with a beautiful aroma of perfume that reminds him of home. Ahh, that's nice. He knows it can't be his aftershave.

Eldridge feels the soft touch of a hand gently massaging the back of his neck as a cold Pabst Blue Ribbon beer is placed in front of him on the table.

"Damn, now that's service."

One of the two girls at the end of the bar has gotten the pilot a beer and moves in for the kill. She slowly slides her slender, healthy body around and settles into the waiting Army officer's lap. She looks at him with her dark, exotic bedroom eyes, and he also can't help but notice her large and healthy breasts that are about to pop out of the top of her very low-cut Oriental gown. The dress has a slit clear up the side exposing two beautiful legs and a perfect hip.

"Fuck me!" Eldridge says, a shocked look on his face.

"Okay," she replies, giggling.

"Damn, Benedict! Some kinda place you boys got here!"

"It'll do in a pinch," Benedict says, "but that's not why the chief set this up. We'll get to the fucking around later. Right now we have business to tend to."

He pauses. "Fuck it! Let's play now and do business later."

"I'll drink to that!" Holland shouts.

So, the meeting is postponed due to I and I: "intoxication" and "intercourse."

As the party's just starting to gain some momentum, four large figures emerge from the hot, humid Saigon street, invading the inside of the dark shadows of Frenchie's. Four Green Berets in all their splendor. Olive drab Army fatigues with all the appropriate patches, jump wings, and gold corporal stripes on their sleeves, pants bloused neatly in their spit-shined jump boots, and wearing their fancy green berets. They look sharp. Talk about contrast next to the guys in the bar. Benedict wonders how they keep their boots looking so good. And the hats! Do they get out a ruler and measure each other to make sure they're on just perfect?

In contrast, some of the men in Frenchie's are wearing SEAL tennis shoes. Some are wearing jungle boots. One guy isn't even wearing shoes. And none of them have their fatigues bloused. But, by God, Benedict thinks, we all have a hat of some kind! Though he's not sure how straight they're wearing them.

The LT has to say, though, that Green Berets fight like they look. Very sharp! As a matter of fact, that goes for the Marine Corps Recon platoons too. Not to leave out the Air Force Para Rescue. They all can fight alongside us any day! he thinks.

"What the fuck you call this!" one of the Army pukes spouts off.

"Looks like the Salvation Army to me!" another one of them says.

"Ya know what, I was just thinking to myself how

sharp the Green Berets are, except for these four fudge packers!" Stinehour blurts out.

"What'd you say?" one of the Green Berets asks.

Little five-foot-six-inch Roten stands up and says, "He said suck my shorts, cunt breath!" And with that, he dives straight down between the closest of the Green Berets' legs and throws a punch straight up into the guy's nuts.

The Green Beret obviously didn't expect that from the little guy. It takes him completely by surprise.

The bar guys, on the other hand, aren't surprised at all. As a matter of fact, none of them even move. They just sit there drinking their beers, watching the event transpire before their eyes as if they're at a theatrical experience of some kind. They do stop playing with the girls, though. It's almost as if they know something the Green Beret guys don't.

Indeed, out of the shadows behind the poor unsuspecting foursome comes six feet three inches of greased lightning. An iron hand shoots to the side of the neck on one, drops him like a stone. A spinning kick to the chest of the one in the middle forces all the air out of his body, dropping him to the floor. Then, in the same smooth movement, he continues to swing around just in time to catch a punch coming in from the other side. He twists in such a fashion as to incapacitate the third aggressor, driving him to the ground and holding him in position with the threat of breaking his arm while he drop-kicks the last guy in the face—the one who'd been doubled over by Roten. Poor Roten only has enough time to crotch shot that one guy before all four have been laid to rest like so much dirty laundry.

As the proverbial dust clears, one hell of a scary figure stands over the four Green Berets, moaning in pain on the floor. He looks like a combination of a fifties reject and a mutant from a nuclear holocaust.

He has a completely shaved-smooth bald head and wears olive drab Army fatigues with the sleeves ripped off, exposing at least twenty-inch biceps. He has a thirty-inch waistline, with fatigue high-water pants that drop over a pair of high-top tennis shoes.

"Who in the hell is that?" Pete Eldridge asks with surprise.

"That, my friend, is Brent Ellison, otherwise known as Animal!" Benedict tells him. "He's with another SEAL platoon that's fixing to go back stateside."

The Green Berets start to stir. As they come around, one of them says, "Who are you guys, SEALs?"

Collier pipes up, "We have a winner!"

"Well, fuck me!" the Green Beret says.

"Okay!" says the girl in Pete's lap.

They all laugh and then join the party.

Once the bar in Saigon is worn out, Benedict invites the River Rats and their newfound Green Beret friends back to the SEAL Team hooch at Nha Be for further overindulgence of the alcohol variety. In the process, they discover that the Green Berets are having the same problems they are: no helicopter support at night or in bad weather.

Eldridge starts to explain: "You see, us Army types have this blue card that we're issued in flight school that has a hole in the middle of it. Our instructor taught us to hold this card up to the sky and look through the hole in the middle and if the sky matched the card, we could fly. If it didn't, we had to stay on the ground."

Stinehour says, "You gotta be shittin' me?" Everyone has a good laugh over that.

Eldridge goes on to explain that about ninety-five percent of the helicopter pilots are not instrument qualified. The instructors are, along with all the fixed-wing people, but not the chopper pilots. Thus, the reason for no support at night or in bad weather.

Eldridge is an instructor, and so has the qualifications, which is why he helps the SEAL Team whenever possible. However, Benedict knows they need help from above on a consistent basis.

You know what happens when you get a bunch of drunks together brainstorming?

They can come up with some pretty good ideas. The one they settle on that night is to pull from the Navy.

"Why don't you get some of those jet jockeys that can land on an aircraft carrier in all kinds of weather and teach them how to fly helicopters?" Eldridge says.

Collier adds, "You know, it's a well-known fact the Navy has the best schools. Why not use 'em?"

Holland jumps in: "We need to make sure they're as committed as the rest of us, though! I mean, part of our family. We don't want just any flyboy up there trying to save our ass!"

"Yeah, that's right!" Roten says. "These guys got to be somebody special that understand our special needs!"

Benedict pipes in, "How you going to manage that?"

Animal, who hardly ever speaks, puts his two cents in: "Besides SERE school, send them to the Army's school at Fort Bragg, then give 'em to the Marines and let them have a shot at 'em. When they've completed that, let the SEAL Team instructors finish 'em off. If they survive that, I imagine we'll be able to count on 'em with no problem."

"That's a great idea!" Eldridge says. "They can be trained by the other branches that already have schools in place. That'll save money and time."

Benedict interjects, "You know that you're talking about something that's never been done before, don't you?"

"A Navy Special Forces helicopter gunship squadron trained by Navy, Army, and Marines," Chief Davis says. "Where in the hell are we going to get the kind of clout to pull that off?"

One of the River Rats who joined in on the get-together after coming in off the river pipes up with "How about Admiral Zumwalt?"

Benedict turns to him, saying, "Sure, how you goin' to pull that off?"

"Well, I couldn't, but my dad probably could."

"How's that?" Benedict says.

"Probably because my dad is Admiral Zumwalt."

You could have heard a pin drop.

With that, the wheels are put in motion to create HAL-3: Helicopter Attack Light Squadron 3.

Otherwise known as the U.S. Navy Seawolves.

4
_____

Washington, D.C., on a Wednesday morning in January 1967. Rain was falling on a cold winter day outside Admiral Elmo Zumwalt's office window. Looking over the latest reports from Southeast Asia had left him depressed. His son had contacted him about the idea of a Navy Special Forces Attack Helicopter Squadron. He knew this definitely had merit. However, it met with a bushel basket full of problems that he was facing.

In an attempt to save money and manpower, the Department of the Navy had allowed Zumwalt to send men from HC-1 in San Diego to go TDY (Temporary Duty) to four separate locations in the Delta region of South Vietnam. Two were on LSTs (Landing Ship Transports) on the Bassac and Co Chien rivers. The other two were land based at Nha Be, just outside of Saigon, and at Vinh Long, farther down in the Delta. The Vinh Long location was where the Army would take care of upkeep and maintenance on the birds (helicopters). That was decided because the Army was supplying the choppers, and thus would do all that went with them. This being the case, the Army required that each helicopter had an Army warrant officer as copilot.

Daniel E. Kelly

Each Detachment—or Det., as they were called—consisted of two helicopters: UH1-B gunships. They had been doing an outstanding job supporting the River Patrol Boats and SEAL Teams, as well as other military organizations. They were earning an impressive reputation, and had put together a very good recruiting film for use back in the states that was going to be shown to new personnel going through basic training. They had picked up the nickname "Seawolves."

Admiral Zumwalt had just come out of a meeting with the Navy Department's "powers that be," and they were not happy. Besides having a seventy-eight to eighty-two percent casualty rate of HC-1, the Army and Navy crews were not getting along. To add insult to injury, with no one person in command of the four detachments, there was a lot of rivalry between the teams at the four locations, causing further challenges.

The result of that meeting was an assignment to create a squadron that would replace the HC-1 crews in Southeast Asia. Admiral Zumwalt was in charge of what would be the first official Navy Attack Helicopter Squadron in the history of naval aviation. The order was open-ended, meaning "Do whatever it takes to give our sailors what they need over there." It's notable that the assignment involved commissioning the squadron in Southeast Asia, not in the United States. That too would be a first.

To make it happen, Zumwalt knew he needed a commander who was self-motivated, knew how to bend the rules without breaking them, and had the initiative to do something that had never been done before—to create a squadron of personnel that was full of piss and vinegar and worked as one united, kick-ass team of cutthroats. In short, they would operate as a cousin of the SEAL Teams.

It was time to stop looking over the bad news and start creating good news. Clearing his desk, Zumwalt asked his secretary to bring him the personnel files he had requested. It was going to be a long, hard job picking the right guy for the mission at hand.

After spending days going through hundreds of personnel files trying to come up with the best choice possible, he'd narrowed the candidates down to five commanders. Focusing on those, Zumwalt began to gather all the additional information he could, including background stuff that is often overlooked.

Commander Larry Barker was one of the five candidates. He was a stickler for detail with a perfect military record and a record as one hell of a helicopter pilot. His present command had a very low accident rate and always came up with an excellent score at inspections. He used to fly Super Constellations.

A second candidate was Commander John Bear, a good-looking self-motivated man who also had a perfect record with great flying skills. Zumwalt met him once at a party, and Bear almost talked his leg off. He had very good people skills and was well-liked by everyone. Before he went to choppers, Bear had been a P5M Marlin driver.

A third candidate was Commander Stuart Carl, a six-foot-five-inch monster who was about as subtle as a freight train. His people skills were lacking, but his men would do anything for him. What was unusual about Carl was that during his off time he would fly to South America and do missionary work with his parents. His experience was with A-1s before going to helicopters.

A fourth possibility was Commander Jacky Car, another great flier with an excellent record. A former jet jockey who switched to helicopters, he was a stickler for regulations. Always went by the book.

Commander Robert W. Spencer was the final candidate. Zumwalt discovered by talking to friends that when Spencer was three years old, his mother had passed away. From that point on he always dreamed of being a naval aviator. In August 1949 he reported for Naval Aviation Training at Pensacola, Florida, and in May 1951 had carrier qualifications. Spencer flew forty combat missions in naval fighters over Korea and was one of the youngest pilots to graduate from the Naval Fighter Weapons School in 1953. Now known as "Top Gun," a good friend of his, Jerry Berry, got him hooked on the Navy's helicopters. Spencer had told Berry that if they could ever put guns on them, they'd really have something special. That was in 1960.

As he climbed the ladder of success with his newfound love of helicopters and gained more responsibility, he began to attack his various new jobs at hand like a fighter pilot would. Back in those days, Navy helicopter pilots had a reputation for preferring to stay away from gunfire.

Spencer put a very large dent in that. He ran his units like attack aircraft instead of rescue helicopters. He was considered a renegade who would do anything to get the job done, even if he had to stretch the rules. His number one concern was always his men. That included the enlisted men. It was said they would do anything for him.

The more Zumwalt dug into this man's past, the more Spencer resembled the *McHale's Navy* kind of guy he was looking for. The admiral had to make one last call before making up his mind, to Captain Charles Karr.

"Charlie," he said. "This is Elmo."

"Yes sir! What can I do for you?"

"Well, I've just about made up my mind on who I'm going to pick for the job."

"Yes sir."

"What can you tell me about Commander Spencer?"

Answering with a laugh, Karr said, "Well, sir, I remember once, a long time ago, he said to me, 'If there's ever a time that the Navy decides to create an attack helicopter squadron, I sure hope I can be its first CO!'"

"Well, Charlie," Zumwalt said. "Why don't you give him a call and tell him he's got the job. HAL-3 is his baby and I want some serious results! Tell him to handpick twenty pilots and a hundred maintenance personnel from our volunteer list. Out of those numbers, we'll see who makes up the combat teams that will be the first Seawolves to take a chunk out of Charlie's butt!"

Zumwalt had heard about the nickname HC-1 had earned and was going to carry that name over to HAL-3.

He went on to say, "Have them report to Coronado for their indoctrination and Special Forces training. After that, send them to Camp Pendelton for weapons training with the Marines. Then cut them orders for Fort Benning to go through helicopter gunship school with the Army."

"Aye aye, sir!"

"I want our enlisted to be able to fix anything on those choppers, blindfolded, by the time the Army instructors get finished with them! I want to have the fastest scramble times, fastest quick turnarounds"— akin to a pit stop in a car race, where the helicopter is reloaded with ammunition, rockets, and fuel, then launched back into battle—"most accurate rocket strikes, and best weapons experts South Vietnam has ever seen!

"Oh, and, Charlie, once they've accomplished that, if any of them want to take advantage of the Army's jump school, authorize that as well. I want these guys to get all the training we can arrange for them before they go into action. The better the training, the faster the results!"

"Aye aye, sir. Will do!"

The stage was set. The orders were cut. History was about to be made.

5

In February 1967, the wheels were put in motion to make HAL-3 Seawolves happen. Commander Spencer had picked his cutthroats carefully, including his XO (executive officer, or second in command), Lieutenant Commander Con Jayburg. Their first stop was Bell Helicopter to decide what would be the best aircraft for the job at hand.

After test-flying the Cobra, Spencer informed the Bell executives that it would not suit their needs at all. The people at Bell were not happy. Commander Spencer explained that from his previous experiences in Vietnam and from the Seawolves job description, they would be responsible for their own medevacs (medical evacuation) as well as the insertion and extraction of SEAL Team members. What's more, he vowed that none of his men would ever be left behind.

That left the Huey helicopter, or UH1-B, as the only choice possible.

So much for Bell Helicopter's big sale of Cobras to the U.S. Navy.

There were already an abundance of B model Hueys in South Vietnam that could be had at a cut-rate price without having to take a big chunk out of the taxpayers' pockets. This was the case because the Army was getting newer C model Hueys to replace the older B models. Commander Spencer had not yet figured out how to commandeer these discarded helicopters, but he would cross that bridge when he came to it.

Now that the decision concerning the helicopters had been made, it was time to move on to the training at Coronado and Camp Pendelton. The West Coast beaches, the Marines, and the SERE (Survival, Evasion, Reeducation, and Escape) school took their toll on volunteers. Those who survived the tough training, under Commander Spencer's leadership, were a serious pack of renegade pirates with a team spirit that was hard to match. The ones who didn't survive were sent back to the regular fleet.

Next was Fort Benning. The U.S. Army was in for a shock. It didn't take long for the Seawolves to make themselves known at this new location.

The Army's base commander and the inspector general were giving Commander Spencer a tour of their facility. As Spencer's hosts drove by the barracks they had so graciously loaned to his aviators, he looked out the window of the car and, with shock, saw a huge flag flying from the top of the barracks that said U.S. NAVY SEAWOLVES.

The base commander, seeing that his guest was somewhat embarrassed by the flag, said, "Hey, don't feel bad, we haven't seen that kind of spirit around here for a long while!"

Leaning back in his seat, Spencer thought to himself that things were coming together just fine.

The tour moved on to the range where the Seawolves would be doing their practice gun and rocket runs. It was an old parade ground that still had the bleachers where people could sit and watch the troops pass in review. Beyond that, there was a very large field on the side of a hill, with a couple dozen old armored personnel carriers scattered around as markers that could be seen from the air. It's what the Army pilots used to focus on to practice their shooting.

The vehicles looked to be in pretty good shape—because they'd never taken a hit from the students. The colonel remarked that the purpose of the range was to teach the pilots how to approach a target area, shoot, and then how to exit the target area. They didn't concentrate on accuracy.

Hearing and seeing this, Spencer resolved to change that situation.

The colonel pointed out that the parade ground was where his ordnance—rockets and machine-gun ammunition—and fuel trucks would be when his men came in with their choppers to reload and refuel in between practice runs.

The tour went on to the hangars, where the sailors would receive their maintenance training on the UH1-B helicopter. The facilities were very impressive. It looked like you could eat off the hangar floor, and the mechanics kept their tools arranged as if they were surgeons. The instructors were very capable too. Spencer could see that the Seawolves would be in good hands.

Later that evening, when he got back to the barracks, Spencer discovered that the entire place had been painted and fixed up like a ship. Everything resembling the Army had been removed. There were Navy pictures hanging on the walls, and the floor was painted like the deck of a ship.

Lieutenant Al Whazalesky had designed and written

up a newsletter, which he'd named the "Wolf Gram." He'd helped himself to a mimeograph machine and paper from a local Army office. They never missed it. The newsletter, was to be sent back to the men's families on a monthly basis, informing them on how their loved ones were doing. Only positive information would be conveyed.

Spencer was impressed. Nobody had told them to fix the barracks or do any of the rest. They all just got together and decided it needed to be done.

After a few weeks of intensive training for the pilots and crews in their various jobs, it was off to the target range for phase two. That's where the bleachers on the old parade ground were, and it was time for another surprise that no one had given any thought to—the flying habits of these young Seawolves and how they differed from the Army.

A pilot landing an aircraft on the rolling deck of a ship in high seas needs complete control. There's no room for error, or he goes for a swim, if the mess-up doesn't kill him. It's the same with IFR (Instrument Flying Rules) flying. In order to put yourself where you need to be—while in zero visibility—it's imperative that your aircraft platform is totally stable. This means flying a perfectly level path through the sky. Naval aviators, trained to do this from the beginning, are used to flying in this manner.

As for how the rockets are fired from these helicopters: rocket pods are mounted on two solid mounts, one on each side of the aircraft, each pod holding seven 2.75 rockets. It means that wherever the helicopter is pointed, that's where the rocket is going to go when it's fired. Keeping that in mind, the pilot has a flip-down rocket sight straight in front of him to look through, similar to sighting down the barrel of a gun. The rocket pods are adjusted or sighted in on the range in the same manner, just like mounting a scope on a rifle.

If a shooter flinches when he pulls the trigger on a gun, there's no telling where the bullet will go. The same thing applies in a helicopter. If the aircraft is jumping and bumping all over the sky, there's no telling where that rocket will go.

The point, again, is to fly completely steady all the way to the target without flinching, just like making a carrier-top landing in rough seas. And this, of course, affects target practice.

The copilots operate a remote control gun sight in front of them that aims four M-60 machine guns mounted outside on two pylons, one on each side of the aircraft, above the rocket pods. In other words, there are two guns on each side. All four face forward and move a certain number of degrees up and down and from side to side on a hydraulically operated swivel mount.

One other thing to note is the role of the door gunners. If the helicopter is flying totally steady, then the gunners are going to be much more accurate in their shooting, as well. They will be shoulder-firing a free-hand M-60 machine gun from the sitting position in the back door, one on each side. Together with the pilot gunners, this spells out a lot of firepower, and success with a capital S.

The Army had set up refueling trucks on the parade grounds in front of the bleachers, as previously instructed. Also, there was a good supply of rockets and machine-gun ammunition so they could practice the quick turnaround—which, again, resembles a pit stop for a race car—and thus fly as long as they wanted. The exercise began with six helicopters, and six Army instructors flying in the copilot seats, plus twelve gunners, one on each side in each aircraft.

Commander Spencer had assigned a very young captain as a teacher: Deek Burger. He was six feet one inch, and rode a Harley-Davidson motorcycle to and from work. Everybody liked him because he was always the life of the party.

Spencer's two gunners were Shawn Godfrey in the left door and Gary Greenhaw in the right.

Godfrey was a five-ten, nineteen-year-old, slender-built kid from Iowa. He was a sharp kid but always seemed to get into trouble in school. In fact, he made E-4, petty officer, third class, in just six months. He was a regular hippie type, and he liked action.

Greenhaw was an E-5, petty officer, second class, a twenty-two-year-old who stood five-eleven. He was a pure kick-ass, backwoods Louisiana boy who lifted weights like a crazed gorilla. He had a thirty-inch waist and twenty-inch arms, and came across as a real live hillbilly.

Lieutenant Junior Grade John Luscher was Spencer's trail bird. His instructor was Captain Patrick Dun, from Texas, a very sharp "by the book" guy. Their two gunners were Don Green and Dan Kinchen. They had joined the Navy together and gone through boot camp together and volunteered for this crazy outfit together. On top of that, they'd raced motorcycles together before joining the Navy. Both were E-4s and loved living on the edge.

The team behind Spencer's two gunships was led by his XO, Lieutenant Commander Jayburg. From Florida, Jayburg was right up there with the best when it came to flying. He also was a by-the-book guy. His wingman was Lieutenant Whazalesky, who had a reputation for doing whatever it took to get the job done.

When they first went up, it was a beautiful morning, with a few white puffy clouds scattered across the sky. The wind was a little gusty out of the south. Liftoff time for the first group to fly rocket runs was 0900. All six choppers were turning up on the flight line, ready for takeoff. Very slowly, three teams of two helicopters each would pull their birds up in the air to about five feet and do what was called a "hover check." Staying in that position, the pilot and copilot would look over the instruments to make sure all was working correctly. Then the flight leader would contact the tower and get clearance for departure to the gun range.

Once that was completed successfully, each pair would slowly tip their bird forward and move down the edge of the runway. As they gained speed, they would also gain altitude. Clearing the end of the runway, it was time to turn toward the practice range area as they lifted farther skyward.

Leveling off at 1,000 feet and on the correct heading, each team would fly in formation as they would on patrol in Vietnam. The trail bird would be staggered to one side or the other of the lead bird, never following directly behind, because otherwise, if the enemy on the ground was shooting at the lead helicopter and missed, they might accidentally hit the trail bird.

Coming up on the practice range, it was time to

land on the parade ground and load up with rockets and M-60 machine-gun ammunition. Again, it would be done in teams of two. The reason for this was that a Seawolf combat team in Vietnam would consist only of two choppers each, so they would get used to that now.

Commander Spencer, being the lead bird in the first group, brought them into final approach to the parade ground, flared, and set the B model down with the precision of a hummingbird. In like manner, his trail bird, Luscher, set his helicopter down at almost the same instant about twenty yards back and just to Spencer's left. Their new Navy crewmen, two per chopper, slowly exited each of the aircraft, as per the lessons their Army counterparts had taught them, and started sliding live rockets into the fourteen empty tubes on each bird. Completing that task, they loaded up their door boxes with 2,000 rounds of 7.62 machine-gun ammunition. That done, they climbed back aboard, loaded their M-60s with the belted ammo, and gave the all clear to their pilots.

With his new load of hardware, Commander Spencer pulled ever so slowly up on the collective, added power, and his UH1-B responded by rising to a smooth hover about five feet off the parade ground. Hover check complete, he slowly nosed his bird forward and lifted into the sky. Luscher was right on his tail and just to his left per instructions. Both birds climbed to altitude and swung around to make their approach to the target area. Spencer, being first in line, started his run at 1,000 feet.

His Army instructor, Deek, said, "Don't worry about these targets out here. They've been out here for years and nobody's hit one yet. We're just trying to teach you the technique of a daisy-chain-type delivery so that you'll get the feel for covering your wingman."

"Daisy chain" meant that each chopper would fire and roll around to cover the other one. While the lead chopper was rolling out from his strike, the wingman would already be firing at the target, in order to cover the lead bird until he was in position to cover the trail bird. Thus, they would be learning how to approach, fire, and exit the area.

Nosing his chopper over, Spencer lined up his sight on one of the nice, shiny, untouched APCs (Armored Personnel Carriers).

Keep in mind the need to fly a smooth platform in which to shoot rockets and guns from. Now, being very careful and exact in the positioning of his bird and his descent, Spencer took aim and squeezed off his first rocket. The 2.75 missile burst from its tube, filling the compartment with sparks from its rocket engine and screaming toward its target on the ground. Before it impacted, Spencer squeezed off another shot. Both rockets, one after the other, slammed into the APC, exploding on impact. Perfect bull's-eye! The gunners in the back were tearing up the targets as well.

Deek Burger freaked. "Son of a bitch!" he shouted as Spencer pulled out of his dive as if he were back in Korea flying his fighter plane.

Luscher came in underneath and put two more rockets right on the same APC.

Burger jumped again, as if shot, because the explosions were so close on their break off to the left. "Jesus Christ, you guys learn fast! Shit!"

As Spencer broke off his run, Shawn and Greenhaw in the back, with their seat belts on, discovered there was a blind spot in the daisy chain. As Luscher broke off his rocket run, Spencer hadn't had enough time to get lined up on the target again. Luscher's ass was hanging out for anyone to shoot at. In contrast, the Army's daisy chain worked well because their gunship teams had three choppers, not two. That way, the lead chopper had time to come around and cover the third one when he made his break.

Shawn Godfrey had to stop firing at the target because he was strapped to the seat. Pushing his ICS button, he said, "Hey, Greenhaw, can you see Luscher behind us yet?"

"No!" Greenhaw replied. "I could if it wasn't for this damn seat belt."

"No shit!" Godfrey said.

"Oh, there he is! I got him now!" Greenhaw said as he opened up with his M-60, sending tracer rounds down at the APC and right under Luscher's aircraft.

"Hey, boss," Godfrey said to Spencer. "We gotta do something about these seat belts so we can climb outside and shoot straight behind us to cover the other bird on break. We got ourselves a serious blind spot going here."

"Okay," Spencer said. "When you come up with something, let me know."

By this time the poor personnel carrier was a mass of twisted metal.

Spencer came around and settled on another nice, smooth approach to the target area. His sights fixed on the same APC, he went after it with a vengeance, punching off four more rockets. At the same time, his gunners were working it over as well. Again Luscher duplicated his boss to the letter. By now the poor APC was looking pretty bad.

It was time for Con Jayburg to do some damage. His team was just as deadly. All three teams were making a shambles of the armored vehicles on the side of the hill.

By lunch they were causing such a ruckus that the bleachers had filled with Army personnel watching the show as they ate lunch. They hadn't ever seen such a display of accuracy with the 2.75 rockets, fired using Kentucky windage.

Jayburg would roll in and *blam!* Another unmarked APC would receive a cosmetic alteration. Then Whazalesky, next in line, airmailed three more deadly darts right under Jayburg's belly as he broke off from his attack. BOOM! BOOM! BOOM!

The crowd in the bleachers cheered and clapped hysterically as another APC became unrecognizable. Every time one of the teams landed and got out to refuel and reload with ammunition, the now standing-room-only crowd gave them a standing ovation.

The exercise went on for several days, as all twenty Seawolf pilots got their turn at the armored vehicles on the side of the hill. The quick turnarounds had also shown incredible improvement. Like an Indianapolis speedway pit stop. The gunners were just a blur as they threw ammunition, rockets, and fuel at their respective aircraft.

It became a regular happening for the Army people to go out to the range and spend their lunchtime watching the display: the rotor blades chopping and popping at the air, the explosion of rockets slamming into steel on the hillside, the M-60 machine guns cracking out their tune, and the roar of the crowd every few minutes, as if a favorite team had just made another touchdown. You would have thought Spencer's pirates were professional entertainers. But they were anything but.

So much for practice.

Now for the real thing.

6

Leaving California and Travis Air Force Base behind, the Boeing 707 leveled off at its cruising altitude. Its destination: Tan Son Nhut Air Force Base in Saigon, South Vietnam. Commander Spencer, Lieutenant Commander Con Jayburg, Lieutenant Whazalesky, and the rest of Spencer's pirate band of Seawolves were settling in for the long flight to that exotic land in the Orient. They were in dress white uniforms, looking sharp and smelling good.

The No Smoking light went out on the overhead, and the Zippo lighters went into action, the nervousness in the air mingling with cigarette smoke. Some were familiar with the war zone, which was officially called a "police action." However, many had not yet been to Vietnam.

There was a notable difference of nervousness among the men. Those on their first trip couldn't sit still, and those who'd been there before were getting into a comfortable position to try and get some sleep. The four gunners—Gary Greenhaw, Shawn Godfrey, Dan Kinchen, and Don Green—were trying to make their way up the narrow path in the center of the plane, toward their fearless leader, "Boss" Spencer. They had something they just had to show him. Pushing and shoving along, pressing past people standing in the aisle talking and smoking or on their way to the bathroom, they finally reached their goal.

Spencer was concentrating on the mission at hand like a father taking a vacation with 120 of his kids and trying not to lose any of them in the process. Not to mention treating each one like he was his favorite. As he went over some notes on the fold-down tray in front of him, he was distracted by a safety belt and buckle that resembled part of a pilot's safety harness—used to strap the pilot into his seat in the aircraft. He looked up and saw Shawn Godfrey holding the belt, and the three other gunners crowded around him in the narrow aisle.

"What's this?" Spencer asked.

"It's the answer to our cover problem, Boss," Godfrey said.

"Yes, sir," Kinchen piped in. "We've been working on it since that first day on the range."

"You bet," Greenhaw said. "Check it out, sir, it's a seat belt harness that goes around your armor-plated chest and then has a three-foot extension that fastens to the bulkhead of the chopper so if ya fall out, you won't go all the way. With this, you can stand out on the skid and shoot under the tail boom to get complete coverage for our trail bird on the break!"

"We had the Army guys in the parachute hangar help us make it," Green said. "Whatta ya think?"

"Damn good idea, boys!" Spencer answered. "You think you can find someone at the airfield in Saigon to help us make some up?"

"You bet your ass!" Green and Kinchen said at the same time, followed very shortly with a meek, "sir."

"Hey, Whazalesky," Spencer said, raising his voice.

"Take a look at this. The kids came up with a pretty good idea. Think you might be able to help 'em out?"

The four gunners made their way back to Whazalesky's seat to show off their new toy.

Commander Spencer finished studying his notes and the overview of what he was going to do once in Saigon and lay back in his seat for a long-needed rest. Ahead of them were eighteen to twenty hours of dull flying as they traveled to the other side of the planet.

On May 5, 1967, the big Boeing 707 bearing Commander Spencer and his gang landed at Tan Son Nhut Air Force Base. Southeast Asia, the tropics of the Orient. It doesn't matter how many times you've been there, that heat still hits you right between the eyes.

Spencer's men exited the aircraft and went down the long portable staircase that had been pushed up to the door of the plane. They stepped onto the hot tarmac and made their way to the terminal building. While enduring a long wait in customs, Spencer had Jayburg arrange transportation to get them to the Meyer Cord Hotel, also known as the Annapolis Hotel. That's where the first Seawolves would be staying until further notice.

As usual, it took the South Vietnamese government and the United States Army forever to get everyone shuffled past the red tape involved in entering the country and out to the waiting buses that Jayburg had scraped up from the local Navy motor pool.

The three old school buses had been painted navy gray, with chicken wire and steel bars welded over all the windows. They were parked in the big circle drive that led up to the terminal building. The pavement was covered with a thin layer of red dust that was common in Vietnam. Each bus had a Navy driver dressed in olive drab fatigues and Army combat jungle boots, with pants neatly bloused inside. Slung behind each of the drivers' seats was an M-16 with a bandoleer of extra clips of ammo. All three men looked confident as they instructed the group to load up and get comfortable for the long ride to their destination.

The men's conversations as they boarded the buses varied from how the trip had been up till then, to the refueling stop they'd had in Hawaii, and the Vietnamese police, who looked like small children to them. They also wondered aloud how soon they could get out of their dress white traveling uniforms, take a shower, and get into something more comfortable. Not to mention where they could get a drink and why in hell was there chicken wire and bars over all the buses' windows.

The veterans were busy answering all these questions, especially the one about the chicken wire and steel bars. It was there to keep the VC from tossing grenades into the bus as it made its way through the busy streets of Saigon. The men were astonished. Do you mean there's VC in Saigon? Welcome to the NFL, rookies!

On the ride from the airport to the hotel, everywhere they looked there were motor scooters of every kind, size, and shape zipping this way and that. Motorized rickshaws carried Vietnamese and soldiers alike, and military vehicles with machine guns mounted on them patrolled the streets. They saw sandbags and barbwire surrounded buildings everywhere, and people moving shoulder-to-shoulder through a marketplace that seemed endless on both sides of the street. Maneuvering their way through the constant traffic jam appeared to take a real artist, or a psycho.

After the three buses had successfully made the trip from Tan Son Nhut Air Force Base to the hotel, Commander Spencer was to report to Admiral Veth, commander of U.S. Naval Forces in South Vietnam. Spencer asked Whazalesky if he would mind taking his bags in and dropping them off.

"No problem, sir," the lieutenant replied. "Don't you worry. I'll take care of everything." Spencer had earned that kind of respect from his men in training back in the States.

With that out of the way, he hung on to his brown leather satchel with his orders in it and commandeered the bus he was already on, ordering the driver to take him to Main U.S. Headquarters. The other two buses returned to the Navy motor pool.

The drive wasn't far. Most of the U.S. military compounds were located a stone's throw from the Saigon River. Main U.S. Headquarters was in an area that included the National Assembly Building, the prime minister's office building and compound, and the U.S. Embassy, all within walking distance of each other. The hotel was halfway across town, by the main PX and commissary.

Spencer had to report in with Admiral Veth and do what was necessary to get HAL-3 commissioned. But he also had some important requests to make of the admiral.

Dodging the locals pedaling bicycles, riding motor scooters, and driving their little taxies was a challenge, but the Navy chauffeur slid through the traffic like a pro driving an eighteen wheeler through downtown

Dallas, Texas, during rush hour. It didn't take him long to find his way to the front gate of Main U.S. Headquarters.

Slowing up to turn into the drive that led up to the front gate of the compound raised a cloud of dust in the dead still air. It took a while to settle once again onto the paved street. Spencer looked around when the driver stopped at the gate to check in with the Army guard on duty.

He saw machine-gun emplacements on all corners of the wall surrounding the headquarters, with barbwire and sandbags, dry dusty streets, and a war-torn city. Would the country ever see any peace? he wondered. It could be a beautiful place to come for a vacation, with all its waterways and all the temples, with their hidden wonders to explore. The possibilities seemed endless, if not for the war.

The driver was checked through, returned a sharp salute to the guard, and they continued down the dusty road inside the compound. Heading for the Navy's office area, Spencer took note of the sweat-stained dress white uniform he was wearing. When he left California, his pants had a clean, white, pressed appearance to them. Not anymore. At least the commander boards on his shoulders still looked good, he thought, and the front of his white short-sleeve shirt still looked fairly decent. The ribbons he had earned from Korea and other adventures were topped off with the gold Navy pilot wings on his chest. A career military man like Spencer noticed things like that and always wanted to look his best. Especially when reporting in with the admiral.

"Here we are, sir," the driver said respectfully.

"Right! Thank you, son," Spencer replied. "I appreciate the lift. You take care now."

Dismounting from the bus with his satchel under his arm, Spencer made his way up the wooden steps and through the double doors of the white, wood-framed two-story building.

Inside, the air-conditioning was a pleasure. The foyer was a two-story open space with two ceiling fans extending down toward the first-floor area. A staircase went up the left side of the room to a balcony that went across the top and disappeared down the hall in both directions.

He walked up to the receptionist at the desk in front of him and asked directions to Admiral Veth's office. And as he did, he heard a familiar voice from the staircase above sing out his name.

"Commander Spencer, I do believe! How the hell are ya?" It was the admiral.

"Well, sir," Spencer responded, "I'm anxious for a clean bed and a shower, to be exact."

"Come on up and we'll get ya a cool drink to tide you over," the admiral said. Glancing over his shoulder, he said to his secretary, Yeoman First Class Petty Officer Karr, "Wendy, would you be so kind as to get Commander Spencer a drink?"

"Yes, sir!" she replied.

Wendy Karr was a petite, spry twenty-eight-year-old from a small town in Wisconsin, with a keen sense of what the admiral needed all the time. She had just finished with the supply inventory and was walking back to her office when he'd called out to her. Quick on her feet, she darted into the break room and retrieved a cool Coke from the refrigerator.

Spencer went upstairs, shook hands with the admiral, and walked with him toward his office down the hall. Wendy Karr caught up with the two naval officers and handed Spencer an ice cold Coke like it was a baton in a relay race. Spencer thanked her with the eagerness of an athlete who had just finished winning that race.

Spencer followed his host into the outer office, where Karr now sat at her desk, and on into a large office that had a panoramic view of the other buildings in the compound and the city and Saigon River beyond. The admiral's desk was centered in the middle of the room, in front of the window, with just enough space behind it to fit his chair.

Admiral Veth asked, "You want anything added to that Coke?" as he made his way around the desk.

"No, sir. Not at the moment," Spencer said from in front of the desk, standing almost at attention. He downed the Coke in a short series of gulps.

"Relax, Spencer, have a seat," the admiral said.

"Yes, sir." Spencer lowered himself into the chair facing the admiral. "I'd like to get at the business at hand, sir, so I can get back to my men." He took a folder full of papers from his satchel, leaned over the desk, and handed the admiral his orders. As he set the empty bottle of Coke down on the desk, he saw with surprise that Wendy Karr was right there to take it from him. She disappeared back into the outer office, leaving the two men to conduct their business.

"I understand completely," the admiral answered as he looked over the commander's papers. "Things are about the same with HC-1 detachments since you last heard," he went on. "Det. One on LST-846, the *Jennings County* on the lower Bassac River, is still having trouble covering their assigned area. It's just way too much space. Det. Two at Nha Be is still getting the shit kicked out of them every time they go into the Rung Sat Special Zone. Det. Three at Vinh Long can't seem to get along with the Army. Plus, they're having the same problem as Det. One. Their area is just too much for them to handle. Det. Four on LST-786, the *Garrett County* on the Co Chien River, of course, is in the same boat as Det. One and Det. Three. The area is just too big.

"Don't misunderstand me—they're all doing a great job. We just need more of them, and I see by your orders that you're adding three more detachments. A Det. Five on an LST on the Ham Luong River. That'll sure make the Det. Four guys happy. A Det. Six land-based at Dong Tam with the forward base of the U.S. 9th Infantry Division. That takes a lot of pressure off Det. Three. And Det. Seven at Binh Thuy with the PBR base is perfect for helping out Det. One. It means we need to get you another LST out of Japan headed this way ASAP. Plus, with these additions, you're going to find yourself short on manpower. We've stepped up recruitment to try and get you more people, but in the meantime I'll see that the HC-1 personnel are transferred to HAL-3."

"Thank you, Admiral," Spencer said. "I appreciate your help. I'd also like to request that my guys be able to skip the usual three days of indoctrination. I know we're supposed to go through it, but given the extensive training we've already had, we could really get a jump on things by using that time doing something more productive like putting together the supplies we're going to need in Vung Tau." He referred to the location that had been picked by Admiral Zumwalt for the home base of HAL-3 and its maintenance support group.

"I know just how you feel," the admiral answered. "I think we can accommodate you there with no problem at all."

Spencer went on to say, "I've dreamed about commanding an outfit like this back as long as I can remember. If you could just see your way clear of giving me a free hand on this operation, I promise you that I'll have our guys water-skiing on that Saigon River out there before my tour's up!"

"Relax, Commander," Veth said. "I've talked to Admiral Zumwalt about this at length, and believe you me, we're both behind you all the way. As a matter of fact, I've done a little research for you with the HC-1 personnel. I've handpicked one of their guys to help you out any way he can. If the rumors about him are just half right, I think you'll be very pleased. He's Lieutenant Junior Grade Henry Boswell III. Everyone calls him 'Pistol.' One hell of a pilot, and all he needs is a high-ranking person like yourself to stick his neck out and back him up. If you want it, he can get it." The admiral paused and glanced out the door behind Spencer, then back at the commander. "I just don't want to know about it." He paused again. "Oh, he's also got Vung Tau completely wired."

"That all sounds great, sir! When do I meet this gentleman?" Spencer asked.

"He's stationed with the HC-1 detachment at Nha Be. I've instructed him personally to use their fire team to transport you down to Vung Tau tomorrow. One of their drivers is picking you up in the morning at 0800 hours."

"Will there be room in the two choppers for a couple more passengers?" Spencer asked. "I'd like to take my XO and another pilot with me."

"That shouldn't be a problem, Commander," the admiral answered as he handed Spencer's orders back to him.

Spencer stood up and took his orders from the admiral, saying, "Thank you, sir, for everything. I won't let you down!"

As the admiral stood up he said, "Oh, and by the way, I noticed that your orders instruct you to report to the senior naval officer in charge once you get to Vung Tau. That's going to be interesting."

"How's that, sir?" Spencer asked.

"Well," the admiral said, "there isn't one. You're it. So I guess you'll have to report to yourself."

Spencer paused and then said, "Okay. At least I know I'll be on time when I do report."

"One more thing, Commander. HAL-3 was commissioned the moment you set your foot on the tarmac at Tan Son Nhut. Congratulations on being the first captain of the first attack helicopter group in the history of the United States Navy."

"Thank you, sir," Spencer replied. "I can't tell you how much I appreciate this opportunity!"

Both men exchanged a few more words, said their farewells, and shook hands once again. Then Spencer exited the office and was met by Karr. "Sir, I have a ride waiting for you out front," she said.

She escorted Spencer back down the hall, down the stairs, and outside to a waiting Army jeep painted navy gray, with a Navy driver dressed just like the others from the motor pool. Spencer walked around to the passenger side and climbed aboard. Karr popped a smart salute to the commander, and he returned it.

This new driver was a twenty-two-year-old second class petty officer named Josh Archer. He knew only one way to drive, as if the jeep were his '57 Chevy back home, a 327 V-8 under the hood with a four-speed Hurst shifter on the floor. He would have described it as "Balls to the wall and God help any Vietnamese that gets in my way." Archer knew Karr, and she'd filled him in on what the commander wanted.

"I'll have you back to the hotel and that shower before you know it, sir," Archer said.

"Just as long as it's in one piece," Spencer answered.

With that, Archer popped the clutch and they were off. They went down, around, and through the streets of the compound, keeping an eye open for MPs, who didn't like speeders—because on a military base you're not supposed to do more than fifteen miles per hour—and out the gate past the Army MP guard. They popped sharp salutes back and forth and on out to the street, with the dust flying. Archer laid on the horn, Vietnamese yelling obscenities as he barely missed hitting them, dodging in and out of traffic as if he were trying to break a previous record going from the Main U.S. Headquarters to the hotel. Spencer just sat back and hung on. A nice shower and a clean bed was what he wanted, just as long as it wasn't in the hospital.

7

Man, is it hot, Spencer thought as he opened his eyes to a new day in Southeast Asia. He sat up slowly in the sweat-soaked bed. The sheets were stuck to him, and he thrust them off in the hope of feeling somewhat cooler. No such luck.

Placing his bare feet on the concrete floor and sitting there for a moment while he gathered his thoughts, he noticed the itching bug bites on his bare back, legs, and feet—not to mention other areas under his Navy-issue undershorts. That was the welcome to Vietnam that everyone enjoyed, regardless of his or her rank or age.

Then Spencer was off to the shower, where there was no privacy at all: mamasans doing their duty, like maids, walking straight through the bath areas without a second thought. He reflected on the cultural differences—that what was embarrassing to Americans didn't seem to bother the Vietnamese at all.

Moving right along, Spencer finished getting cleaned up and put on the work clothes he would wear for the rest of his tour: olive drab fatigues neatly bloused inside black jump boots, fatigue top done up with labels over each breast pocket. One said U.S.

NAVY, just above which were embroidered gold-colored Navy pilot wings, and the other label had his name. And on each collar were embroidered silver oak leaves signifying his rank as commander. The finishing touch was his black beret. This was to be the standard uniform for all Seawolves from now on.

Lieutenant Whazalesky walked in, suited up and ready to roll. He said, "Good morning, boss. The XO is already downstairs with hot coffee for us."

"Outstanding!" Spencer replied. "Is Luscher and his crew ready?"

"Yes, sir."

Spencer had already assigned a pilot and copilot and two gunners to Det. Two, which meant they would be accompanying them on their trip to Nha Be.

"Then let's head on down, we've got a lotta work to do!" Spencer said.

They proceeded to the elevator and took a short ride to the lobby. The XO, Jayburg, met them with two cups of hot coffee.

The night before, Spencer had filled them in on what was going to take place this morning.

Lieutenant Junior Grade Dick Stout, from New York, was the kind of guy everyone liked right away. He was five-ten, had an average build, brown hair, and brown eyes. Friendly George Sappenfield was a five-foot-nine blond-haired Kansas farm boy whom everyone called "Sappy." Redheaded Terry Reasoner was five-foot-seven and from Oklahoma City, and had a quiet look about him that said, "Don't fuck with me." Reasoner always kept his cool in tough situations.

Whazalesky opened the conversation with "Green-

66

haw, Shawn, Green, and Kinchen have already got a ride back out to Tan Son Nhut air base earlier this morning to meet up with someone I lined them up with. Hopefully, this guy can help them out with their new invention."

"Yeah, they were pretty excited about getting that done," Jayburg said.

That brought a big smile to Spencer's face. It was the kind of initiative and teamwork it would take to pull the mission off.

"That's good," he said. "Let's hope they can find someone to make enough for all our gunners by the time we're ready to rock and roll."

When he joined the Navy, Lieutenant Whazalesky had remained in touch with one of his school friends who'd joined the Air Force. They had both become pilots, and his friend, as luck would have it, had been stationed out at the air base here in Saigon for about six months. He was flying C-130s—a four turbo-prop engine cargo plane that paratroopers would jump from. Calling ahead, Whazalesky had set up a meet, through his friend, with a Green Beret sergeant who might help Greenhaw, Godfrey, Green, and Kinchen get those harnesses made.

The four men went through the gate at Tan Son Nhut base in the back of an Army 2.5-ton truck, heading for the parachute rigger hangar to try and meet up with U.S. Army Green Beret Sergeant David Gritzner. With no canvas top on the back of the truck, the view was much better than the one they'd had in the Navy bus they rode in on from the base the day before. Four pairs of eyes were darting here and there, trying to take everything in like a thirteen-year-old boy in a whorehouse. As the tour continued through the dust-covered paved streets, they passed barracks, Quonset huts of all sizes, and all sorts of different-shaped wooden buildings, but all painted the same color—white with green trim.

Continuing on to the hangar area, they heard jet engines of all kinds, sizes, and shapes. They passed a C-130 starting up its engines on the flight line, and off in the distance a Boeing 707 was accelerating down one of the runways, heading back to "the World." Straight above them, three F-4 Phantoms were passing over, flying in formation. It was one hell of a busy place.

As the scenery started to change to Army aircraft, such as the C-7A Caribous, Bird Dogs, UH-34s, Chinooks, and finally the Army Huey helicopters, the men knew they were getting close. Sure enough, the truck made a sharp right, went between two hangars, around the back, and came to a stop in front of the parachute rigger hangar.

"Here ya go, boys," the Army driver yelled out.

"Thanks, man!" Shawn Godfrey said as all four leaped out of the back of the truck.

Green turned around and asked, "How do we get back to the hotel?"

The Army driver said, "I'm headed over to pick up some supplies at our depot. It'll be about an hour, and I'll come back by here and pick you guys up then. Is that going to be long enough?"

"It should be," Green answered. "Thanks a lot. See ya in an hour."

There they all stood, in front of the door, decked out in their olive drab fatigues, their pants neatly bloused inside black jump boots, name tags and naval insignia above each breast pocket of their shirts, embroidered in black. On each collar were pinned black plastic Navy stripes signifying their ranks, and above the U.S. NAVY on their chests were gold-embroidered Navy aircrew wings. To top it off, they wore black berets.

Green was the first through the door, the harness they'd made back home held tightly in his hand. Kinchen, Greenhaw, and Godfrey followed. They all lined up in front of the counter, looking around to see whom they needed to talk with.

An Army spec four got up from his desk and said, "Can I help you folks?"

"I sure hope so," Kinchen said.

"Yeah, we're lookin' for a Sergeant Gritzner," Green said. "Our LT called ahead and set up a meet with him."

"He was just up here a minute ago getting a cup of coffee. He's probably out back," the spec four answered.

"Is it okay for us to go out there?" Green asked.

"Sure, man. They're just packing chutes. Come on, I'll show ya!"

They walked around the counter, followed their Army guide down a hallway lined with offices on each side, and moved out to the hangar, where men were packing chutes on big tables.

"There he is, over there," the Spec four said, pointing across the hangar to a doorway that opened up onto the tarmac.

The four walked across the hangar building to the

figure standing in an open doorway. The sergeant had noticed them about the time they were halfway across. He stood about five-foot-ten, was slender, clean-shaven, and looked to be about twenty-five years old.

Head to toe, he was impressive. His fatigues were pressed, his pants bloused inside spit-shined black jump boots, the sleeves on his olive drab top rolled up just enough to show his bulging biceps. He had gold sergeant strips, a Special Forces shoulder patch, silver jump wings, and a green beret sitting sharply on his head. He held a cup of coffee in one hand and a cigarette in the other.

Before any of the four could say a thing, Gritzner barked out, "You guys the Seawolves I'm supposed to get with this mornin'?"

"You bet!" Godfrey answered.

"I'm Staff Sergeant Gritzner," he said, held out his hand, and greeted each of the four with a hearty handshake. "You boys are some crazy motherfuckers! Saved my ass more than once! Whatever you need, if it's within my power to get, you got it!"

The four young greenhorns were taken aback by this greeting. Back at Coronado, their training had covered the reputation the HC-1 had in Vietnam, but it was still a surprise to get such feedback firsthand.

Greenhaw said, "What we need is a whole shitload of these made up for us," and pointed at what Green held in his hand. With that, Green presented the harness they had made.

"Where'd you guys get that?" Gritzner asked.

"We had it made back home," Godfrey said.

"No shit!" Gritzner said with a laugh. "Let me show ya somethin'."

He flipped his cigarette out onto the tarmac, followed by tossing what was left of his coffee, and walked toward the Army jeep sitting just outside, next to the hangar. "Come on, get in," he said to the puzzled foursome.

Kinchen, the largest of the four, jumped in up front, while the other three loaded themselves into the back.

With Gritzner driving, they flew across the tarmac and out onto the flight line. They zipped past a bunch of aircraft and down to some Army Huey gunships that were parked in a long line, each with their own sandbag revetments, which resembled miniature garages with no tops, the walls on three sides made up of sandbags that rose about waist high. They came to a screeching halt in front of one of the choppers.

"Here, come over here," Gritzner said.

They all piled out and followed him over to the helicopter. Gritzner pulled back the crewman's door on the side of the aircraft and pointed out a rig that was clipped onto the back bulkhead of the compartment where the gunner sat.

"Is that what you need?" Gritzner asked.

"Well, I'll be damned!" Godfrey said. "That's exactly what we need!"

"No problem, boys! How many you want?" Gritzner asked.

"As many as we can get!" Kinchen said.

"Where you guys going to be based out of?" Gritzner asked.

"Vung Tau," Green answered.

"I'll tell ya what—give me a couple days, and I'll have a crate of 'em shipped down to ya. How's that?" Gritzner asked.

All four answered with great excitement, saying it would be outstanding and very much appreciated.

Sergeant Gritzner took them back to wait for their ride, then left.

As the four stood waiting, they expressed relief that they hadn't said anything about coming up with a new idea. They felt silly, but at least they'd accomplished what they'd set out to do.

Back at the hotel, the five officers and two aircrew were still waiting for their lift to Nha Be. Finishing their second cups of coffee, they were wondering how much longer it would be. The question was answered as fast as they had thought of it.

Henry Boswell III walked in through the front door and into the lobby where the HAL-3 personnel were standing. "Good morning, gentlemen," he said, removing his Marine Corps olive drab hat. He walked up and shook each man's hand. "They call me Pistol Boswell," he told them.

"You're right on time, 0800 hours on the dot," Spencer said as he looked at his Navy-issue watch. "You usually this punctual?"

"Not hardly, Commander. I just got lucky," Boswell said.

After Spencer introduced everyone, Jayburg asked Boswell, "Would you like a cup of coffee before we leave?"

"No, thanks. I had my fill before I left to come get you guys," Boswell answered, and with that, he led the seven out front to their waiting taxi.

What they saw before them was a Ford panel van with no windows, painted brown. Or at least as well as could be determined through all the dirt.

Their driver was one of Pistol Boswell's aircrew,

Tim Brooks. He was an Iowa farm boy, five-foot-nine and wiry. He jumped out of the driver's seat and ran around to the back of the van to open it up and help load the luggage.

As the two side-by-side doors opened, what Spencer and his crew saw before them was a surprise: fold-up lawn chairs, several M-16s with bandoleers full of extra magazines—the clips filled with bullets that went in the guns—and some wooden boxes.

"Your chariot awaits," Boswell said.

"What's with all the firepower?" Luscher asked.

"Oh, that's in case we run into trouble between here and Nha Be," Boswell answered.

"You've got to be kidding," Jayburg said.

"Hell no. We run into shit all the time between Saigon and Nha Be," Brooks said. "It's pretty rough territory between here and there."

"Well, isn't that good news," Spencer said humorlessly.

The group piled in the back and made themselves comfortable in the lawn chairs. Pistol Boswell got in the front seat next to Brooks, who would drive. As they pulled away from the front of the hotel, Boswell reached into a cooler sitting between him and Brooks and pulled out a cold can of beer. "I don't suppose any of you would like some breakfast," he asked as he handed one to Spencer.

"All right!" Spencer said. "The breakfast of champions!"

The cool ones were passed around, and those who had cigarettes lit up.

As they sat there, leaning to and fro with the movement of the van sliding this way and that, dodging traffic, Luscher grew curious about the wooden crate sitting next to him. "Hey, what's in the box back here?" he asked.

"Oh, that's just a case of grenades," Brooks answered without losing a beat in his driving and drinking. "You never know when you might want to toss one out the window," he said, laughing.

"Holy shit," Jayburg said.

And the van full of cutthroats whizzed on out of the city and down the one-lane highway through the jungle, headed for Nha Be or bust.

8

Arriving at Nha Be forty-five minutes later without incident, the brown Ford van passed through the Vietnamese navy base, past the U.S. Navy PBR base, and on into the HC-1 section.

Passing through that gate, looking to the right, three Quonset huts were surrounded by sandbags neatly stacked up to the bottoms of the windows, with a break in the sandbags for the front door. The first hut housed the enlisted aircrews, the second the pilots and SEAL Team officers. The third hut was for the SEAL Team platoons that would rotate out back to the World every six months.

To the left, two revetments with sandbags were stacked up to chest level on three sides, leaving the forth side open, facing toward the Quonset huts. The space was left so the helicopter could hover out, sideways, to take up a position for takeoff. There were two UH1-B gunships parked in them, fully loaded with rockets and M-60 machine guns. On the tail boom where u.s. army used to be painted in small black letters, it now said u.s. navy. Also, all the doors had been removed from the helicopters to lighten the load, so they could carry more ammunition.

The runway was between the huts and the gunships.

The hard-packed dirt went straight out about fifty yards and stopped at the edge of the Saigon River. Because of the fence and buildings behind them, the gunships would always take off toward the river.

The van pulled up in front of the middle hut and stopped. Spencer and his group piled out, and the HC-1 officer in command of the Nha Be detachment, Lieutenant Commander Jack Bolton, came out of the BOQ (Barracks Officer Quarters) to meet them.

Pistol Boswell made the introductions, then he and Brooks excused themselves. They had to start the morning's preflight inspection on their aircraft, and it had to be done immediately because they were to take three people down to Vung Tau. Sappenfield and Reasoner went along with Brooks so they might be of some help, and also for some OJT (on the job training).

Meanwhile, Spencer, Jayburg, Whazalesky, Luscher, and Stout got acquainted with Bolton and some of the others who made their way out of the barracks.

Bolton had black hair, dark skin, a husky build, a tattoo of a skunk on his arm, and he always had a smile on his face. He was a "Mustanger," which meant that he'd begun as an enlisted sailor and worked his way up through the ranks, eventually becoming a lieutenant commander. In fact, Bolton could have been a captain, but he was a cutup from way back, and he got into trouble all the time. He could have been the original Commander McHale.

Bolton and his crew had already done their preflight while Boswell and Brooks were doing their taxi run to Saigon.

Lieutenant Junior Grade Stuart Joynt, the SEAL

Team One platoon leader, joined in on welcoming the new head honcho. Joynt was a six-foot-five-inch, 225-pound monster man, a "whoop ass," Fort Worth Texas cowboy. He was one of the Seawolves' biggest fans.

The whole place became a buzz of handshaking, welcoming the commanding and executive officers of HAL-3. It was short-lived, though, because Spencer wanted to get to Vung Tau right away. As soon as Pistol Boswell and Brooks, with the help of Sappenfield and Reasoner, finished their inspection of their aircraft, things started to settle down.

Pistol would be flying the trail bird with his copilot, Lieutenant Junior Grade Mike Dearborn, from Louisiana. Spencer and Whazalesky would be in the back, sitting between the gunners, Brooks and Carson. Carson was a black man from Houston, Texas, built like a gymnast.

The lead ship's pilot was Bolton, and his copilot was Lieutenant Junior Grade Henry Conners, from Detroit. In the back of their chopper, with their gunners, were Jayburg and a second HC-1 pilot, Caeser Juneau, from Chicago. The extra pilot had to come along because Pistol would be staying in Vung Tau to help out Spencer. The fire team—which is what the two gunships were called—would be flying a regular patrol on its way back to Nha Be. That meant they would need another pilot.

It was time to load up and head for Vung Tau. Everyone started donning their gear. It consisted of the Mae West orange inflatable life vest worn under the bulletproof vest, in case they went down in the water; armored vests; sidearms; and the flight helmet. As far as the clothing they wore, it varied as much as everyone's personality. Pistol had changed out of his clothes he'd worn into Saigon and was now wearing olive drab fatigue pants that had been cut off to make shorts. His top was a regular olive drab fatigue short-sleeve shirt. The only thing that stayed the same was his black jump boots. The other pilots and crew were a mixed and matched mess of tiger-striped fatigues, olive drab fatigues, SEAL Team swim shorts, and Navy flight suits. They resembled the sailors in the movie musical *South Pacific,* and they had the weather to match.

Spencer and Whazalesky were in Pistol's chopper, sitting on the flex gun trays between the gunners. Brooks was out in front of the bird, holding on to the main rotor blade, waiting for Pistol to start it up. Carson sat in the right door, with his M-60. Dearborn was in the copilot seat on the left, and Pistol in the pilot seat on the right.

Pushing the intercommunication button on his stick, Pistol spoke to Spencer and Whazalesky: "You gentlemen ready back there?"

Spencer pushed his intercom button, which was part of the cord going into his helmet, and said, "Affirmative!"

"All right, boys. Here we go." Pistol yelled out the door that wasn't there: "Coming hot!"

The jet engine whined as the turbines began to rotate. As the pitch of the engine got louder, the pull on the main rotor blade out front got stronger. Brooks held on as long as he could, until finally the blade was pulled from his hands. They did it this way so a gust of wind wouldn't surprise them, blowing on the main rotor blade and making it act like a teeter-totter, banging in one direction so hard that it could damage the rotor head. By the time the rotor was pulled from Brooks's hands, it would be turning at a sufficient speed to keep the teeter-totter effect from taking place.

With the rotor blade turning at a safe speed, Brooks took his place in the left door. Plugging his helmet into the radio system, he hit his floor button and said, "We're all clear back here, sir."

"Roger that," Pistol responded.

Moments later both birds were turning up at full speed. Spencer looked out front between Pistol and Dearborn and saw Bolton's bird rise up off the ground about five feet into a hover. The pitch of the rotor blades changed as Pistol slowly pulled up on the collective. The blades popped louder as they took a bigger bite out of the air, throwing it down and in turn raising the helicopter up to about five feet. Spencer listened intently as the radio communication between the two birds continued.

"Seawolf Two-three, hover check complete," Pistol said.

"Seawolf Two-six, hover check complete," Bolton said. "Moving to the right."

The first number in their call signs had a special meaning, indicating that it was Detachment Two. The second number signified the speaker's rank within the detachment, "six" being the highest. So naturally, the detachment commander was a six.

With that, both birds, hovering, moved slowly to the right until they were centered on the short dirt runway. The dust they raised was minimal, due to the regular activity of the choppers.

Spencer, still watching and listening closely, saw

Seawolf 26 tip his bird slowly forward and accelerate down toward the Saigon River, lifting easily into the sky, but only about twenty or so feet. Boswell did the same. Pulling up a little more on his collective and pushing the cyclic gently forward, his bird also moved down the short runway and climbed out to about twenty feet. Then both birds played follow the leader as they made a sharp turn and headed downriver.

Spencer turned one way and then the other, checking out what the gunners on either side of him were doing. Both men had their M-60 machine guns up on their shoulders, ready to fire at a moment's notice. He saw that they had lost altitude and couldn't have been more than five feet off the water while doing better than 100 knots. Looking forward again, he could barely get a glimpse of Seawolf 26 out in front. The chopper was bobbing this way and that, whistling around and in between large cargo ships going up and down the river. He had to look up to see the bridge on a passing ship.

Both helicopters continued screaming downriver, just missing sampans and junks going to and from market. The Seawolves were taking a ride that would beat anything at Disneyland as they moved down toward the coastal waters.

Once they reached the halfway point between Saigon and the coast, the two gunships made a sharp left-hand turn off the river, up and over the jungle's edge. The jungle here was so dense, they couldn't see the ground. And now, instead of cargo ships, they were dodging around trees. Occasionally, a skid would slap at the top of one of the palm trees they went over.

Pistol came over the intercom system, saying, "Hey, Skipper. This place we're flying over is the famous Rung Sat Special Zone. I bet there's been more action here than the whole country."

Spencer pushed his button and said, "I've heard of it before. Is it really that hot?"

"Seawolf Two-six, Seawolf Two-three. Over," Pistol said.

"Seawolf Two-three, Seawolf Two-six. Go ahead," Bolton answered.

"Seawolf Two-six, Seawolf Two-three. My rider wants to know if this area is really that hot. Over."

"Seawolf Two-three, Seawolf Two-six. Let's have a little show-and-tell. Follow me!"

"Roger, Seawolf Two-six." With that, the lead bird started to climb out from their low-level run, and Pistol was right behind him.

Breaking through 600 feet, Spencer heard a sound he hadn't heard since Korea, like firecrackers going off. Except these firecrackers were accompanied by green tracer rounds zipping passed the front window between the two gunships. As Bolton and Boswell kept climbing toward 1,000 feet, the gunners in both birds answered the ground fire with four M-60 machine guns blasting away.

Spencer and Whazalesky were showered with hot brass, ejected from the gunners' M-60s on both sides. The experience for the two officers in back was eye-opening.

Once the two birds had broken through 1,000 feet, the firing stopped. Moments after that, the Seawolf gunners stopped as well.

Pistol hit his intercommunication button again:

"That's why we call the area between three feet and one thousand feet 'the Death Zone.'"

Whazalesky said, "Roger that! How about us staying above one thousand feet the rest of the trip?"

"We can do that," Pistol said with a laugh.

9

Arriving at Vung Tau, the first priority was to find a place to spend the night. Spencer checked with the local U.S. Army brass and got an invitation to sleep at their BOQ on cots in the hall.

Next on the list was to send a message to the four detachments, notifying the commanders to report in to Vung Tau for a meeting with the new skipper at 1500 hours the next day. The meeting would be held at the local Officers Club.

The third thing that they needed was transportation and a place they could call their headquarters. That assignment was given to the scrounger, Pistol Boswell.

He had no problem with it. He just got on the horn and called in some favors from the local Australian outfit. They had an old mobile home trailer they were using for storage, and had it pulled over to a spot close to the base chow hall. It was just a stone's throw from the PSP runway where Spencer hoped to have his squadron hangar. Another plus was the fact that the Aussies were storing sheets, pillowcases, pillows, and blankets in the trailer. They also threw in a window air-conditioning unit.

Concerning transportation, Pistol did his magic. He thumbed a ride up the road to the local PBR base and commandeered a patrol boat and crew. Through radio communication, he knew there was an LST coming out from Saigon that had an old Navy pickup in the cargo hold. Pistol had cut a deal with the captain, which consisted of trading a genuine captured VC flag for the truck. Riding out into the shipping channel on the patrol boat, he intercepted the LST, boarded her, and finalized the deal. Once the captain had his flag, it was a small matter for him to drop the pickup off on the Vung Tau beach.

That was just the first day. Needless to say, Spencer was impressed with Pistol's ability to make things happen.

On the morning of the second day, Pistol had heard about an unfinished hotel lying stagnant two klicks down the main road, off the base. After gathering up the men's ration cards for hard liquor, he purchased a truckload of Black Label Jack Daniel's along with some other grade A brands of booze and took a peace offering to the "Dragon Lady" who owned the vacant building. After the wheeler-dealer had done his thing, they had their own BOQ with twenty rooms, with an unfinished roof and wall around the villa. They also needed work done on supplying power, electrical lighting, and plumbing.

This was easy enough to remedy, though. Pistol called on Ensign Burke from Nha Be, who used to be a CB—a Navy Seabee, or Construction Battalion, as in the John Wayne movie *The Fighting Seabees*. Burke flew down from Saigon along with some of his old CB friends and they finished the hotel. It was proudly named the Seawolf Manor.

Before they'd even arrived in Vung Tau, Pistol had also found an Army barracks that was unfinished. It was located just behind the mess hall. He got the Army to trade him that building if he could supply a new shower facility for their men. Once again, that was not a problem, given the CB connection in Saigon.

By the time Spencer's meeting at 1500 hours was ready to take place, Pistol had already put all these wheels in motion. It wouldn't be long before Spencer and his crew would have a respectable home to live in.

At meeting time, all were present and accounted for at the O Club, having a burger and a beer. The stories were flying. To Spencer, it sounded like a contest for who could tell the best battle stories. There was a lot of competition between the four detachments.

He opened the meeting by recognizing Pistol Boswell for all that he'd accomplished for the outfit in such a short period of time. Pistol responded with a statement that stuck in Spencer's mind. He said: "Hey, Skipper, you're just going to love it out here! All you gotta do is fly and shoot!"

Afterward, when Spencer excused himself and went to the latrine, Pistol's words kept pounding in his mind. That's not right! he thought. That's not how it's done. It's not that simple. Slowly and deliberately, he took something from his pocket, looked at it intently for a moment, then pinned it on his chest above his gold Navy pilot wings. It was an old sheriff's badge he had brought from home.

Spencer returned to the table, where his men were still drinking and trying to outdo each other. Standing, silent, he slowly got everyone's attention. They noticed the badge he was now wearing. In a soft tone he began to speak.

"Gentlemen, I just want to let you know that there's a new sheriff in town," he said. "Starting right now, you are all members of the first Attack Helicopter Squadron in the history of the United States Navy. HAL-3 Seawolves will go down in history as being the most successful, the most decorated unit in the Vietnam War. What you've done thus far with HC-1 has been remarkable, to say the least. However, I intend to change the casualty reports we've been getting back in Washington by a very large margin. There's only one way we'll ever get rid of our seventy-eight to eighty-two percent casualties, and that's by having a system that we all follow—or you won't be flying. It's a system that's been tried and proven for many years. When I was flying missions in A-1 Skyraiders over North Korea, we used the same system and it was very successful. There's absolutely no reason to think that it won't work here.

"First off, we must operate as a team. The only competition I want to see is how well you can compliment your neighbor on how much better he's doing than you are. You should never care who gets the glory, as long as the job gets done. A well-done job reflects on all of us, as well as a bad job. We should always be uplifting each other. If Det. Three needs help, we should be killing ourselves to do whatever it takes to see that Det. Three gets that help, no matter if it's supplies or fire support. The only competition I want to see is with yourself. Can you beat what you did yesterday?

"There will be guidelines you must follow on how to approach a target, how to change up your approach, what's the safest way to exit a given target or targets. This will all be discussed at length, and you will take it back to each of your detachments and teach them how.

"Another thing—we're going to repaint all the tail booms in the squadron. I want to see very large bold white letters spelling out 'Navy' on both sides of the tail boom. A bright target for that green NVA out there will be what he shoots at, not just the helicopter in general. If he's aiming for those big bright white Navy letters, what do you think he's going to end up hitting? That's correct! He'll either miss you altogether or he'll hit the tail boom, which has the least amount of vulnerable parts.

"One more thing—we're adding three more detachments. Det. Five will be on the LST-821 *Harnett County,* which is en route from Japan as we speak. It will be on the Ham Luong River. Det. Six will be located at the forward base of the U.S. Army's 9th Infantry Division at Dong Tam. Finally, Det. Seven will be located with the PBR Base at Binh Thuy. What we need from you gentlemen is experience. Pick a few of your best to go with the guys that we brought with us, to get these new detachments started. The faster we get going on this, the more PBR sailors and SEALs we're going to save.

"Do you know what the major complaint is about what you've been doing? Well, the major complaint is, there's not enough of ya! With these additions, we should put a major dent in that complaint. That's seven detachments, fifty-six men, and those fifty-six men are going to leave a serious mark in history!

"Now let's make our attitude as one, and go out there and kill as many of the bad guys as we can and save as many of the good guys as we can, together!"

Spencer's speech pumped the group. He went on to tell them that they would be getting together on a monthly basis to see how things were progressing. He also said that he and Jayburg would rotate out one week each month and fly with a different detachment every time. That way, he could tell how everyone was doing and have some personal contact with all the men.

There was still a lot of work that had to be done. The enlisted men's barracks had to be completed. Seawolf Manor had to be finished. The new shower station had to be done for the Army. They needed more helicopters for the three new detachments, plus M-60 machine guns, rocket pods, pylons to hang the rocket pods on, and a whole shitload of other stuff.

Before the meeting broke up, Jack Curtain came up with the insignia for the new squadron. He'd seen it on a can of Lowenbrau beer he was drinking. The seawolf or lion or whatever it was on the can was perfect. All he had to do was add a trident to it to signify the Navy, then a shield with a spade on it to represent Death, and put red and yellow colors on the shield to represent Vietnam. His idea for an emblem seemed to pull the group together. It would be theirs and nobody else's.

Then Pistol made the suggestion to bring the enlisted men down to Vung Tau. He said they could be a great help in getting things done, and that they could rough it in the unfinished barracks with no problem. It would motivate them more to make things happen.

When they were brought down, in response to his suggestion, Pistol set a good example and stayed with them.

It would be discovered later that Pistol Boswell had it in mind to have his own "Hole in the Wall" gang, like Butch Cassidy and the Sundance Kid. The things they did would be nearly unbelievable.

10

It was another beautiful day during the dry season in South Vietnam. Whazalesky and Pistol were standing on the PSP runway at Vung Tau, waiting for a C-130 from Saigon to land. The rest of the enlisted men and officers were on board.

"Here it comes," Whazalesky said, pointing at the C-130 turning on final approach to the runway.

"All right!" Pistol said.

The big bird, its four turboprop engines whining, came slowly down toward the end of the short PSP runway. Just clearing the busy street, then the fence line, it flared, and the short, fat tires squealed in pain as the plane's weight settled onto mother earth.

The U.S. Air Force pilot at the controls hit the brakes, reversed the pitch on the propellers, and gave it full throttle, making the nose of the large aircraft dip abruptly as the airplane slowed. Pulling up almost to a complete stop, the pilot got off the power and reversed the props to their normal position. He taxied past the waiting officers and went around to the Vung Tau terminal. As he shut down the four jet prop engines, the large ramp in the rear of the aircraft slowly descended, exposing the cargo hold within.

Whazalesky and Pistol ran around the corner, catching up to the C-130 in time to see Greenhaw, Godfrey, Kinchen, Green, and the rest of the enlisted men and officers disembarking. They had a lot of extra boxes besides their Navy luggage. Upon questioning, the group said the contents of the boxes were another donation from Green Beret Sergeant Gritzner. Besides safety harnesses, there were bulletproof vests and other miscellaneous flight crew equipment.

Evidently, Gritzner got some of his buddies with the U.S. Army 1st Cavalry Division and units of the 9th Infantry Division to chip in. The four detachments of HC-1 obviously had a lot of very grateful friends around the Mekong Delta area of South Vietnam.

While Pistol went to get the Navy pickup to carry the cargo to its proper storage location, Whazalesky filled the men in on what would have to happen before they had a place to sleep.

Earlier that morning an Army Sikorsky helicopter CH-54—nicknamed the "Flying Crane"—had dropped off a conex full of lumber by the unfinished barracks. The wood and its transportation had been a gift from Army Captain Pete Eldridge, out of Saigon. So the men had their work cut out for them.

They needed a roof on the place, for one. Also, stairs to get to the second floor. Not to mention walls. The building had been framed up and included a second floor, but no stairs, just ladders. On top of which, they had no beds or mattresses. Pistol had a line on these, but they were locked up in a warehouse owned by the U.S. Air Force on the other side of the base. However, "Butch Cassidy" had a plan. The trick was to get the "Sundance Kid," Whazalesky, to go along with it.

After walking the men over to the construction site and making several trips with the pickup to transport all their things, it was time to draw up the plan of attack. While the maintenance men worked on the barracks under the watchful eye of the ex-CB and now naval aviator, Ensign Burke, the aircrew guys with Pistol would do a reconnaissance of the U.S. Air Force storage facility. That would be in preparation for a covert operation to take place under cover of darkness that night.

Burke's other CB friends were still working on the BOQ just off base. So, the officers who came in on the C-130, with the enlisted men, made their way down to help with finishing the sleeping quarters.

While all this activity was taking place, Spencer kept a photographic record to use as a tool for badly needed help from Admiral Veth. It included the repairs being done on the BOQ two klicks off the base and the construction going on at their own barracks. After getting all the photographs together, Spencer sent the batch up to Saigon for the admiral to review.

Once the admiral had seen the pictures, he ordered a CB detachment to Vung Tau to complete the BOQ correctly, finish the enlisted men's barracks, and build the shower stalls for the U.S. Army, to complete the deal the Seawolves had made.

But before all this took place, the "Hole in the Wall" gang would pillage the U.S. Air Force storage facility. What they'd discovered on their daytime reconnaissance was that the metal Quonset hut that had the beds inside was in the back of an aircraft boneyard where shot-down or mortared planes and helicopters were kept. It was a holding tank of sorts, until the powers that be decided what to do with the twisted remains.

Further scouting of the area revealed three old

UH1-Bs sitting in the back. They were next to the target building and appeared to be in fair condition. One more interesting thing was spotted: an Air Force tug used to pull aircraft in and out of the hangar. The plotters wondered if it worked, but they would have to wait until that night to find out. The last and most important thing they noticed was that there were no guards. All right! This, Pistol thought, was going to be a snap.

Returning from the daytime scouting trip, Pistol put the plan to Whazalesky.

"Are you sure we won't get caught?" Whazalesky asked.

"Hey, no problem, man!" Pistol answered. "It's going to be a snap! Trust me!"

"That's what I'm afraid of," Whazalesky said. "All right, but be careful!"

The strike was on. Meanwhile, Spencer had made a deal of his own. He'd talked with an Army bird colonel about a certain hangar that was located behind the base PX—the retail supply store and restaurant. It didn't seem that the hangar was being used. Spencer found out the reason was that it was intended for overflow repair jobs when the normal hangar space couldn't handle the workload. It was decided that when the Army moved a repaired bird out, Spencer could move one of his in.

When Pistol heard about this, he got excited. Now he had a place to put the three helicopters and the tug that he planned to snatch that night.

Nightfall, and it was time for the small band to depart for the far side of the base. Whazalesky had talked one of the Army's warrant officers into letting him borrow two tugs, on the ruse that he needed them to tow two of their helicopters to hangar. The ostensible reason they needed to be towed was that they were not flyable yet, which was almost the truth.

Pistol had gathered up his men—Greenhaw, Godfrey, Green, Kinchen, and a guy named Dean Clark, from Florida. There was also an old biker from California, Dave Tarver; an aircrew man, Jeff Lance, from South Dakota; and Tom Talamantez, from New Mexico. These eight were the strongest and quickest gunners in the group. Pistol, Green, and Godfrey were in the front seat of the truck, Tarver and Kinchen in the back. That left Greenhaw and Lance on one tractor, Talamantez and Clark on the other.

They all headed out at about 2200 hours, keeping their lights off so as not to draw attention to themselves as they drove across the air base. The people in the control tower couldn't see them, so they had to be careful as they crossed over runways: all they needed was to have a plane crash into them!

They made it to their objective without incident. As they had taken note of earlier, there were no guards around. Perhaps since it was a relatively dark area of the base, no one thought guards were necessary.

With limited lighting, the men were glad they'd brought red-lensed flashlights so they could see what they were doing. The drive in through all the wreckage stacked up on both sides was tedious, and would be more so on the way out, with all the stuff they'd be taking.

When they reached the Quonset hut, everyone dismounted and spread out to keep watch. Pistol and Kinchen moved up slowly with red-lensed flashlights in hand. Kinchen also had bolt cutters, which he'd borrowed from an Army spec four, telling him he needed them to get into his sea bag, that he'd lost his key and had a tough lock on it. The bolt cutters in the hands of a brute like Kinchen made short work of the padlock on the door.

Six men went into the building, leaving Jeff Lance and Shawn Godfrey outside to keep watch. The intelligence reports had been accurate. The place was full of metal bunk beds and mattresses. The beds needed to be put together, which was perfect because they'd be easier to load onto the pickup outside.

"Well, let's not just stand here," Pistol whispered. "Let's get 'em all loaded up."

The men worked as fast as they could. It would take a lot of beds to fill the barracks, and they only had one pickup, a fact that seemed to occur to all of them at the same time, because everybody stopped and looked at each other as if connected by ESP. It was almost laughable. Then Tarver said, "Hey, we can load a ton of stuff in the three helicopters that we're pulling back with the tugs."

"Yeah, that'll work," one of them whispered, and they all started to work again.

Tom Talamantez broke off from the group loading and went to check out the Air Force tractor. Good news. It ran great. "It must be there for towing shit in and out of the boneyard," he said. He also found the things they needed for hooking up the third chopper to tow it.

Once the pickup was loaded with as much as they safely could pile in it, and maybe a little more, they moved all three tugs into place and hooked up the three helicopters. As they started loading the choppers with beds and an equal number of mattresses, Godfrey signaled that someone was coming.

He'd heard a big truck approaching. It sounded like an Army 2.5-ton, but he couldn't see. Then it stopped. Still nothing. After a while he gave the all clear, and the others went back to work.

About five minutes passed. Pistol had tossed another mattress to Greenhaw, who was stuffing it into the backseat of one of the choppers, when it happened.

A deep voice, in a normal tone, said, "What the fuck do you guys think you're doing?"

Pistol nearly dropped a load in his britches. He turned around in the direction of the voice, which was close by his ear, and came face-to-face with the most frightening thing he had ever seen.

It was a black and green camouflaged face from hell. It was Lieutenant (j.g.) Stuart Joynt and his SEAL Team platoon. They were all around, and none of the Seawolves noticed them until they moved.

Joynt said, "What the fuck you guys doin'? You guys tryin' to be SEALs or what?"

"Jesus Christ, Stuart!" Pistol said. "You scared the shit out of me!"

"Aren't you glad we're on your side?" Joynt replied.

"You bet your ass!" Tarver said with a big smile.

"What are you doin' here?" Pistol asked.

Joynt answered, "Well, we brought you guys down a surprise, except you weren't around. Whazalesky told me what you all were doin' and where. It didn't take too long to figure out that there was no way you had enough help or transportation to pick up all you were going to need. So . . ." He paused, and the Seawolves could hear a 2.5-ton Army truck start up, sounding like it was just around the corner. ". . . I brought some reinforcements."

About then, the truck was backing up. The rest of the SEAL platoon was grabbing things and tossing them in the back.

Pistol turned to Joynt. "Where did ya get the truck?" he asked. "I know you didn't drive it down from Saigon."

"Well," Joynt said, "we found it. That's it, we found it. And would you believe it, the keys were in it and everything. Damnedest thing I ever saw."

With the tone of a father who didn't believe a thing his son was telling him, Pistol said, "Where did ya find it?"

"Oh, it was just sittin' out in front of this ARVN [the Vietnamese Army] barracks all by itself. And would you believe it, it was already running. Damnedest thing I ever saw."

"Holy shit, Stuart. Are we going to get caught?"

"Are you kidding?" the SEAL answered. "No way! Relax, we'll have ya back to the barracks and unloaded in no time. Besides, I got a real surprise waitin' for ya back there."

"I can't wait!" Pistol said.

The loading continued. Joynt had brought four guys with him, and it wasn't long before they had all the beds they needed. Three tugs pulling helicopters, one Chevy pickup, and a deuce-and-a-half Army truck all made their way across the base with their lights out. Mission accomplished.

Arriving at the enlisted men's barracks, they were able to unload what they needed in a short time, with all the maintenance personnel to help.

"Hey, Stuart, what's the surprise?" Pistol asked.

"You mean besides that big cooler of beer sitting over there?" Joynt said, pointing.

"Yes, besides that," Pistol said.

"Follow me." Joynt started for the other end of the barracks.

The two men walked down an aisle of sailors building beds and moving mattresses to an area containing numerous wooden boxes. Then Pistol asked, "What's all this?"

"Well, let me show ya," Joynt said. He pried open the top of one of the boxes, exposing some M-60s.

"Jesus, are all these boxes full of guns?" Pistol asked.

"They sure are," Joynt replied.

"Where in God's name did you get 'em?" one of the Seawolves who'd followed in their wake asked.

Joynt said, "Don't ask."

"That's fine with me," Whazalesky said.

Then it was off to the BOQ to unload their beds. Also, they'd pulled the three helicopters over to the hangar that had been allotted them. The men were up all night, organizing their sleeping quarters and drinking beer.

Sleeping in was the order of the day since no one had gotten to bed until 0600 hours.

Once everybody had caught up on sleep, it was business as usual. They got to work stripping the brushed-on paint off the three choppers, chipping about 350 pounds of paint off each one, or so it seemed to them. All the instruments were intact, but that was about it. The three gunships were going to take a lot of work before they could go back into combat. Luckily, the maintenance people were miracle workers.

Finally, it was necessary to get the last of the miscellaneous parts and tools, to finish off the birds they'd obtained. To do that, they traded beer. The only beer the Army could get was Ballantine, and the Seawolves could get any kind of beer they wanted, like Budweiser or Schlitz, which made the Army guys very happy.

Admiral Zumwalt had cut a deal with the U.S. Army to trade two Navy P-2V Neptunes for four UH1-Bs in good condition. The Neptunes were like new, but the four Hueys weren't. But at least there were now enough choppers to add the three more detachments. And the supplies the Seawolves got from the Army in other than respectable ways precluded complaints. What's more, the hangar the Seawolves were supposed to share ended up being theirs, because once it was filled with gunships, it became a matter of possession being ninety percent of the law. One night, the men painted the whole place navy gray and hung a big sign up that said: HOME OF THE SEAWOLVES.

The Air Force was helpful too. One day, Dave Tarver and Tom Talamantez decided that the skipper needed his own jeep. They got one when nobody was looking, painted it navy gray, and put new numbers on it. Later, they discovered that it was the Air Force inspector general's personal transportation. Talk about bad luck!

But in fact, if it hadn't been for Whazalesky, Pistol Boswell, Stuart Joynt, and the "Hole in the Wall" gang begging, borrowing, or stealing, it would have taken the Seawolves a lot longer to get the project off the ground.

Shortly after everything was in place at Vung Tau, the LST-821 *Harnett County* was in position on the Ham Luong River for Detachment Five. The forward base of the U.S. Army's 9th Infantry Division at Dong Tam had allotted a space just off their PSP (metal) runway for Detachment Six. And the PBR base at Binh Thuy was instrumental in getting a helicopter pad and two mobile home trailers set up for Detachment Seven. With the addition of HC-1's crews to HAL-3, all seven detachments were operational.

Now it was time to kick some VC ass!

11

To the best of my knowledge the following story about four true unsung American heroes—John Abrams, Jim Romanski, Ray Robinson, and Dennis Wobbe—is true. The information was gathered with the help of the Navy SEAL Team, and some of it was corroborated by Chuck Bagley, Lyle Nimmo, and Fred Record. Since some of the information was sketchy, I put it together as best I could.

The silence of the Bassac River was shattered when the loudspeakers on the LST *Jennings County* sounded the scramble bell. It was followed by these words echoing through the ship: "Scramble the helos, scramble the helos, scramble one, scramble one!"

A "scramble one" meant that U.S. troops were in trouble. A "scramble two" meant U.S. and Vietnamese troops, and a "scramble three" was just Vietnamese troops.

Lieutenant John Abrams from Wisconsin, a great leader; Lieutenant Soto, a big, crazy Cuban who feared no man; Lieutenant Junior Grade Jim Romanski, from Portland, Oregon, who loved his work; and Lieutenant Junior Grade Chuck Bagley, who was always fun to be around, were eating their lunch in the wardroom. Sliding back their chairs abruptly from the table, the four pilots hit the door and were out into the passageway that led to the flight deck.

In the chow hall were Ray Robinson, known to the others as "Robbie," and Dennis Wobbe. Using their shoulder-fired M-60 machine guns, the two could take out a VC in a second from 1,000 feet. They had just sat down to a lunch of hot dogs and french fries. So much for that idea. Leaving their trays on the table, they flew out the door and hit the flight deck in a dead run toward their gunship. Lyle Nimmo, a typical surfer type from California, and Fred Record, a good-looking *GQ* type whom everyone called "Buddy," had already eaten and were leaning up against their gunship when they heard the alarm. They were another pair you didn't want to mess with.

All eight Seawolves were dressed according to their individual tastes in combat gear. It could be a Navy flight suit with SEAL Team trunks underneath, or just olive drab fatigues, or tiger-striped fatigues. Each crew member had either a Smith & Wesson .38 Special or a Colt .45 automatic in a shoulder holster, or it was strapped to their hips, as they would have been with old Wild West gunfighters.

The team was on standby alert because their brothers, the SEALs, were in the jungle close by. The "scramble one" could only mean one thing—their brothers had made contact with the enemy.

In about sixty seconds Abrams's bird, Seawolf 15, was turning up to speed. Romanski, Robbie, and Wobbe were in place. Soto, of Seawolf 14, had his team ready to turn up as soon as 15 cleared the flight deck.

The wind from Abrams's rotor blades was pushed against Nimmo as he stood holding on to his rotor blade, waiting for 14's jet engine to pull it from his hands.

As Seawolf 15 lifted off and went over the side, dipped down toward the river water below and then up as they gained speed, the blast of air decreased against Nimmo just as his jet engine pulled the rotor blade from his hands and started spinning. Soto had timed the starting of his bird perfectly, as usual.

Nimmo jumped in his seat just as his helicopter lifted from the deck. As he placed his helmet on, Soto was backing the chopper up to take a run at the other side of the ship. This was done to gain as much lift as possible before going over the side of the LST's flight deck.

By the time Nimmo had the barrel of his M-60 machine gun in place and locked down, they had already accelerated across the deck, dipped over the side, and were climbing up to meet the other Seawolf gunship.

When you scramble, you don't wait for the usual "We're all clear back here, hover check complete, can we go now" bullshit. It's more like "Get the engine started, get the fuck in, and we're outta here!"

Once Abrams was airborne he was on the radio getting tuned in to the SEAL platoon's PRC-25 radio. That way, only the SEALs on the ground and the Seawolves in the air could communicate with safety. No one else could hear what was going on, especially not the Viet Cong. Charlie was famous for having a radio tuned in to what was being said. With the PRC-25, communication was scrambled, so our guys could operate with the knowledge that Charlie couldn't listen in.

Abrams, after getting the radio set up with the SEALs on the ground, hit his button and said, "Stingray, Stingray. Seawolf One-five. We are en route. ETA four mikes. Over."

"Seawolf. Stingray. Roger. We are under heavy fire from the northeast of our position. We will pop red smoke in three, I say again, three mikes. Over."

"Roger, Stingray. Three mikes. Red smoke your position."

Romanski had the flex gun sight turned down in front of him, ready to open fire. Abrams had the rocket sight turned down in front of him as he looked for the first sign of red smoke. Robbie and Wobbe had their M-60s up and ready as they sat halfway out their door with one foot on top of the rocket pod. They were screaming across the river about five feet off the water, heading for the location of the SEAL platoon. As Wobbe stood on his rocket pod, he turned and looked to see how far back Soto was. He could see him way back, just coming over the side of the LST. Hitting his floor mike button with his foot, he said, "One-four is off and coming up, sir."

"Roger that," Abrams said.

Soto was pushing his chopper hard to catch up. Nimmo and Buddy, leaning out with their M-60s ready, could almost swear that the rotor blade was going to cut a little ridge in the river because Soto had them pushed over so much. He was pulling all the power the jet engine could muster. When it was the SEALs, you didn't wait for nothin'.

Abrams came to the edge of the river and pulled his gunship up and over the tops of the palm trees lining the bank of the jungle. He was so low the skids slapped at a few treetops as he sped toward his goal.

Weaving this way and that, dodging taller trees, Wobbe and Robbie kept their eyes peeled for the first sign of their friends on the ground. Knowing they were headed into a shit storm, they couldn't keep the smiles crawling across their faces as Abrams gave them a ride that beat any roller coaster they could ever have imagined. A 110-knot wind blew against their bodies as they hung outside the helicopter, their machine guns pointed forward as they waited eagerly to pull the triggers and make a difference in that crazy war.

Romanski, his flex gun sight in front of him, and ready to kick some butt, had made a mental note of what a beautiful day it was when something drew his attention. Among the few white puffy clouds in the sky, he noticed three specks of something orbiting over the top of where the SEALs were supposed to be.

Hitting his intercommunication button, he said, "Hey, what is that up at about eight hundred feet above our guys?"

Abrams, too busy dodging treetops, left the question up to Robbie and Wobbe. The two gunners, squinting, were trying to develop an opinion on what it was. As they got closer it became clear that it was an Army gunship team on patrol.

At about the same time, it hit everyone what they were looking at. They also started noticing tracers flying over the treetops out in front of them, off in the distance. It was in the same location as the SEAL Team.

All of a sudden, Robbie yelled out over his radio, "Holy shit, sir. They just dropped a green smoke grenade!"

Abrams, still keeping his attention on his flying, said, "Who dropped a green smoke grenade?"

Romanski came back with "Oh, my God, that Army gunship team did, and it's headed straight for our guys! They're receiving fire from the VC on the ground but they don't know that our guys are down there too!"

"They're coming around and rolling in on the SEALs' location!" Robbie said.

"Seawolf, Seawolf. Stingray. Have you noticed a green smoke grenade that just penetrated the canopy above us? Over." The SEALs went on to say, "Break, break, have you noticed Army gunship team rolling in on our position? Over."

All this time, the VC were shooting at the Army gunships as well as the SEAL Team. Talk about dumb luck—out of the whole damn Delta that the Army could fly over, they had to pick this spot at this moment.

Soto came over the air and said, "One-five, One-four. We are attempting to switch off the Prick-25 channel and locate the Army's frequency. Over."

"Roger!" Abrams said. Pushing his ICS button, he went on to say, "Boys, we've run outta time! Get your guns ready! The shit's fixing to hit the fan!" With that, he pointed the chopper right at the tracers coming up out of the jungle. Romanski, Robbie, and Wobbe all got a look of terror on their faces as it dawned on them all what Abrams was about to do.

The lead Army gunship was coming down, getting ready to unload a bunch of rockets right on the SEAL Team. They thought they were all VC. Abrams, coming in fast and low, pulled back on the stick and raised the collective, making his bird climb out to about 200 feet. He flaired and came to a stop in a hover, effectively blocking the charging Army gunships from the

SEALs on the ground. However, doing that put him right over Charlie's position. Talk about hanging your ass out to dry!

The shit didn't just hit the fan; the whole damn manure factory fell on it. No one even bothered to say they were receiving fire. That would have been redundant. Wobbe, Robbie, and Romanski had all the M-60s going without even letting up on the triggers. They could hear loud banging sounds as hundreds of rounds tore through their helicopter's skin. Holes were being torn in the floor and the roof as the bullets came up from the jungle beneath them. The pucker factor was so high in the Seawolf chopper that you couldn't have gotten a number two needle up their butts with a ten-pound sledgehammer.

The SEAL Team had popped their red smoke, so Abrams's gunners knew exactly where not to shoot.

The lead Army gunship, seeing the Navy gunship blocking him from his target, broke off the attack and at the same time saw the SEAL Team's red smoke. Also simultaneously, Soto came up on the Army's radio frequency and filled them in on what was going on.

Abrams, seeing that he had successfully halted the Army, nosed his bird over and exited the area in rapid fashion. Guns still a-blazing as they got down to tree-top level, they accelerated back up to speed.

Soto, with his usual on-the-spot reaction, had popped up too, about 300 feet, and punched off three rockets, sending them swooshing down into the jungle, where the SEALs had wanted the strike in the first place. Wobbe and Robbie, still hanging out their respective doors and shooting like a couple of madmen, could feel the blasts as the three darts found their way through the jungle to the waiting VC below.

Romanski scanned the instruments, expecting to see trouble. Amazingly, there wasn't any. All was working well except for the rotor blades whistling. They tend to do that when a lot of holes are punched through them.

Abrams climbed back up to attack altitude, and Soto pulled into formation behind him. Now that they had some communication with the Army gunships, they were able to blow the shit out of the jungle and Charlie. There were five gunships now—three Army and two Navy—uprooting jungle everywhere. Man, what a daisy chain!

With all that firepower coming down from the sky, it didn't take long to change the situation that the platoon on the ground had been in before. They were able to continue with their original mission, and captured a very large arms cache. And it gave the guys in the air a great body count.

Extraction went off without a hitch. Two Army UH1-Ds—much larger helicopters that are designed to pick up troops—came in and picked the SEALs up as planned, along with all the weapons they had captured. As it turned out, the three Army gunships were just what the doctor ordered, due to the significantly larger force the SEALs on the ground ran into unexpectedly. However, the SEALs were happy campers that Abrams and his crew showed up when they did. As the lieutenant of the platoon said afterward: "Abrams, Romanski, Robbie, and Wobbe must have balls that go clank!"

12

At 2200 hours on a beautiful, clear night, the temperature was around 100 degrees. Lieutenant John Abrams was standing out on the flight deck looking up at the stars. He could hear the gentle splash of the Bassac River on the side of the LST-846 *Jennings County*. It was anchored just north of Doung Island, where the night's mission was to take place.

All the preflights had been done in preparation for the fishing trip. It was going to be like trolling for that elusive blue marlin. Only this would be for Viet Cong.

The bait was the lead gunship flying at about 400 feet with all his lights on. When Charlie raised his ugly head and opened up, little did he know that the trail bird would be rolling in from 1,000 feet above. He'd be flying totally blacked out and would air-mail some 2.75 rockets onto Charlie.

Tonight it was Abrams's turn to fly lead chopper. Lieutenant Soto was flying the trail bird. He could fire a rocket through the eye of a needle, so Abrams didn't mind being the bait, knowing that Soto was covering his butt.

It was time. Lieutenant (j.g.) Romanski, Abrams's copilot, made his way to the flight deck. Everything was lit up with typical red lights, giving it the feeling of Christmas. Abrams's faithful gunners, Robbie and Wobbe, followed close behind. Following right behind them were Nimmo and Buddy. They were the gunners for crazy Lieutenant Soto and his copilot, Lieutenant (j.g.) Chuck Bagley.

It didn't take long for everyone to find their respective places. Nimmo untied the main rotor blade from the tail boom and walked it around the front of the aircraft, as did Wobbe. Buddy and Robbie put the flex gun barrels in and the contacts down on the rocket pods. Abrams fired his bird up first.

"Clear!" he yelled out his door, followed closely by "Coming hot!"

The jet engine slowly came to life. As the pitch got louder, Wobbe had a harder time hanging on to the main rotor. Finally, it was pulled from his hands, and around it went, faster and faster. Robbie was already set in his door, ready to rock and roll. Wobbe jumped in his door and plugged in his helmet to the intercom system, then he hooked up his seat belt and harness. Next, he stuck his barrel in the M-60 he had already placed in his lap, hit the floor button to activate his mike, and said, "We're clear back here, sir."

"Roger that," Abrams came back.

Slowly pulling up on the collective to increase the pitch of the main rotor blade, the helicopter started becoming lighter than air. The metal skids scraped as the weight was taken from them, and the spring action pulled them toward each other. Then came a little wobble signifying that they'd cleared the bounds of mother earth and were headed skyward.

As Abrams backed up to get more room to run at

the other side, the gunners hung on tight, knowing the fantastic roller coaster ride was about to begin. Over the side Seawolf 15 went. They dipped into the darkness and slowly came back up again as they gained speed. What a ride! Robbie was thinking.

All that could be seen from Soto's chopper now were the running lights of Abrams's helicopter getting higher and smaller as he climbed out away from the *Jennings County* and into an orbit around her, waiting for Seawolf 14 to lift off.

That wouldn't be long now. Soto yelled out his door, "Clear! Coming hot!"

Nimmo held on to the rotor blade as long as possible. He had a look on his face that made it seem he was trying to hold on a little longer each time, as if someday he might win. But with all that jet engine, he would lose every time.

Then away it went, the rotor blade spinning like crazy. Nimmo jumped in his seat, got everything in place, looked over at Buddy to make sure he was ready, and hit his button. "All clear back here, sir."

"Roger," Soto fired back.

After their hover check and trip back up to the other side, they moved forward over the edge of the flight deck and dipped into the darkness, then up into the night air. Soto slowly caught up to Seawolf 15 and moved in behind him while Abrams was still orbiting the ship.

"Seawolf One-five, One-four," Soto said.

"One-four, One-five. Go ahead," Abrams answered.

"One-five, One-four. We're on your six o'clock."

"Roger, One-four. We're en route."

Abrams turned south toward Doung Island with all his running lights on. Soto kept all his off, in case someone was watching from the shoreline. That way they'd believe that Abrams was all alone.

The plan was to fly a regular patrol over Doung Island, except it would be flown at 400 feet with all lights on. The enemy would think he was by himself and decide: if the silly American wants to do that, then far be it from us not to shoot his ass out of the sky. In fact, it was an exercise in who was the dumbest.

Abrams slowly brought his bird down to 400 feet just before he crossed over the shoreline of Doung Island. The weather was perfect. There was no moon out, which was a definite plus. He kept his speed up so it wouldn't look too obvious. He didn't want to outrun that blue marlin, and at the same time didn't want to make him suspicious either.

Soto, Bagley, Nimmo, and Buddy were scanning the darkness below. The pressure was almost unbearable, eyes darting around the darkness, trying to get a first look at the muzzle flash in order to pinpoint a target. Then their buddy could turn those fucking lights off quick. Talk about playing with fire. Jesus!

Seconds seemed like minutes and minutes seemed like hours. Unfortunately, this was the only way to take the fighting to the enemy. The only way you could beat Charlie was to change the rules on him, make his backyard yours. If you fought him on his terms, you'd lose every time.

The sweat was pouring off the eight teammates as every muscle stayed tight, ready for anything. They knew they couldn't daydream, or they would be the reason their brothers went to sleep permanently. They had to keep looking, and not fly too close behind. They had to have enough room to nose her over and punch off the rockets. If they were too close, they'd overfly the target, too far back and they wouldn't be able to hit them fast enough to keep their comrades from being shot down. Everything had to be perfect.

Damn! Soto was thinking. I didn't think this island was this big!

Bagley had his trigger finger all set on his flex guns. At the push of a button, four M-60s would send 700 rounds of 7.62 a minute down at the muzzle flashes that would be trying to kill his friends. He was glancing at the instruments and glancing down at the lead ship, with all its lights going, and glancing into the dark jungle below, all at the same time. Bagley was thinking, Shit, I don't have time to think.

Nimmo was leaning way out his door with his M-60 tucked up tight on his shoulder. His barrel was pointed toward his friend's colorful display of running lights as it traversed along, looking as natural as could be. He was thinking, Come on, you son of a bitch, show yourself and I'll blow you into the next world.

Buddy was leaning out his door with his M-60 up and ready for anything. Okay, Charlie, he thought. Do something. Anything. The blood is starting to drain out of my hands, holding this heavy son of a bitch up here like this.

Abrams was flying the lead ship as naturally as possible as he waited to be shot at. He was thinking, Take your time, look natural. This ain't no big deal. As soon as the shit hits the fan, I cut the lights, break to the right, and dive for the deck.

Romanski was all set with his flex guns, in case he got a shot out the front of the bird—in fact, the only direction he could shoot. He was thinking, Keep watching those instruments. Look for muzzle flashes out front that I can shoot at. And, Charlie, just don't shoot me in the butt or the head.

Robbie was holding his M-60 up at the ready, thinking, Come on, you zipper head, I dare ya. Come on, give me somethin' to shoot at. He was so tense he didn't even notice the sweat running off his face.

Wobbe was ready with his M-60. His arms were turning into rubber. It was hot as hell and he was saying to himself, Nimmo, Buddy, you boys better be ready. We're going to catch us a big fish tonight!

The patrol dragged on. The Seawolves were getting edgy. Everyone was starting to think Charlie had gone to bed early that night. It seemed he didn't want to play.

But some things never change. About the time you think it's a bust or you let your guard down, that's always when the shit hits the fan.

All four gunners' arms had just about had it, holding up the heavy M-60 machine guns. Then the sky lit up with red and green tracers. It was like the Fourth of July, and all the bottle rockets were pointed at Seawolf 15. In the helicopter, it sounded as if someone had thrown a whole string of firecrackers on the deck that were all going off at once.

"Jesus Christ, receiving fire, receiving fire. One-four, we're receiving fire!" Abrams yelled over the radio.

"Roger!" Soto came back as he squeezed off the first of four rockets. He already had his ship pointed down at the clear-as-day targets that sat right in front of him. Nimmo, Buddy, and Bagley were hosing down the jungle on both sides of 15. That was six machine guns turning out 700 rounds per minute.

Seawolf 15 was getting fire from both sides, not just

one. They had him set up pretty good, but Wobbe and Robbie were kicking their ass with their M-60s. It's amazing what you can do with the proper motivation. They had a sudden renewed strength in their arms as they skillfully went from one muzzle flash to the next, throwing a volley of machine-gun fire down as Abrams killed their running lights, broke off to the right, and took her to treetop level. And not a moment too soon either.

Soto's first rocket exploded just to the left of Robbie. It was so close he could feel the blast. Abrams's crew had to stop shooting now because they were low and fast, exiting the area. Once they had gotten to a safe distance, they'd hook up with Seawolf 14 and continue the attack.

The VC were surprised by the second helicopter. They had no idea where to shoot. Wave after wave of green and red tracers coming up from the jungle below were flying aimlessly into the empty sky.

Soto had broken off his attack and was waiting to set up behind Abrams as soon as he got up to altitude. Meanwhile, Nimmo and Buddy were still shooting to keep the VC engaged. That way it wouldn't be hard to line up on them a second time.

"One-five, One-four," Soto said.

"One-four, go ahead," Abrams said.

"One-five, I'm coming up at your three o'clock," Soto said.

Wobbe hit his ICS button. "I got him, sir. He'll be in position in a second."

"Roger that," Abrams said. He continued, "One-four, One-five. Make it four darts with a left break. Over."

"One-five, One-four. Four darts, break left," Soto said.

Down they both went, with just their top running light on so they could see each other and not shoot themselves out of the sky. Abrams was taking fire as he broke through 700 feet and started punching off his four rockets one at a time, trying to place them in a nice tight pattern. Romanski was burning up the flex guns, along with Wobbe and Robbie. They all knew they had caught a blue marlin this time because shit was coming right back up at them as they kept pushing on the attack.

Abrams punched off his last dart and broke left. Right on cue, Soto's first rocket hit the jungle with a huge explosion that Wobbe felt. He kept on shooting, though, as they exited the area. Robbie was standing way outside on the skid, shooting under Soto as he completed his run.

Climbing back up to altitude, the team lined up for another run from a different direction. They would follow the golden rule: never do an attack run the same way twice.

"One-four, One-five. Four darts. Break right," Abrams barked out over the radio.

"Roger, One-five. Four darts. Break right," Soto answered.

Down they went again, guns blazing. The rockets were lighting up the night sky as they exploded into the dark jungle beneath.

There wasn't nearly the same enemy fire coming back this time. However, Abrams wanted this fish mounted, so they hit her one more lick before calling it quits.

"One-four, One-five. Salvo the rest and break right."

"Roger. Salvo and break right," Soto answered, as he was thinking, Hey, boss, I only got two left to salvo. You got six.

That's always a pretty sight, though. When you salvo at night, it's real colorful. That's when, whatever you have left, all goes at once. Sparks filled the cabin, with all the rockets clearing the tubes at one time. The four gunners had already changed barrels once and they were white hot again. One more time like this and the gunners would be out of ammo too.

Breaking off from the last run tired the men, and they headed for home. No one shot back on the last strike. Nevertheless, the pilots made a note on their maps as to the exact location for future reference. Since it was such a clear night, the stars were bright enough to see where they were without a problem. It was a different story if you were in the jungle look-ing up.

The deck of the LST lit up, and all the red lights at night looked pretty. Seawolf 15 came in first. The deckhand, his flashlights raised, directed Abrams into the perfect spot to set down. Dropping the collective ever so slowly, the skids underneath spread back out under the weight of the helicopter coming down on them.

Robbie and Wobbe jumped out as Abrams shut the engine down. He then started pulling on the rotor blade brake, to stop it from turning as soon as possi-ble. That way, Robbie could hook it up and tie it down to the tail boom so Soto could come in and land. When Robbie accomplished that, Soto made his approach. He hovered over the flight deck, following the deckhand's instructions, and set his bird down smoothly.

Once all was secure, Wobbe drew everyone's attention to the fresh bullet holes in his tail boom. It was the least dangerous place to get it, but it was a badge of honor of sorts.

Abrams said to Soto: "With all the shit we got out of that particular area, we should probably notify the SEAL Team. I just bet they'll want to plan an operation to see what's down there. It had to be somethin', to justify Charlie putting up that much lead."

That made sense.

It was a big night for the Seawolves, and there was a lot more to come for SEAL Team One.

13

The next day, Seal Team One came down from Bien Thuy on their support craft, dubbed *Mighty Mo*—a Mike boat that had been modified for their special needs. The front of the craft had been welded up with some steel plating, plus more steel plate on top of that, for deflecting B-40 rockets. There were three .50 caliber machine guns mounted on each side. On the front was an 80mm mortar, and on the top of the floating home base there was a 106 recoilless rifle, which was like a rocket launcher. All gun emplacements were surrounded with sandbags. Located forward, underneath the recoilless rifle, was the cabin that contained a comfortable living space for the SEAL platoon. On the rear of the craft, a deck was covered with a canvas top. Sandbags also encircled that. The whole craft was like a floating tank.

Moored on each side was an LSSC (Light SEAL Support Craft): a small fiberglass boat that carried a squad of SEALs and two Special Boat Squadron sailors. M-60 machine guns were mounted on each of the four corners, with the driver located in the middle of the most forward position. The LSSC had a radar dome sticking up in the middle of the boat, for nighttime navigation, and was powered by two 427 V8 motors with dual four-barrel carburetors, which gave it rocket speed on the river.

Also moored on one side of the Mike boat was an MSSC (Medium SEAL Support Craft)—a fiberglass boat like the LSSC but a little bigger. It was designed to carry a platoon of SEALs and two Special Boat Squadron sailors and was almost as fast as the LSSC.

Towing these three craft, with their armor plating, guns, sandbags, and supplies, *Mighty Mo* would only do about six knots, with the throttle wide open.

The large SEAL support craft pulled alongside the LST *Jennings County* and docked next to the many PBRs that were also based there with the Seawolves.

Lieutenant (j.g.) Stuart Joynt, Chief Petty Officer Brent Ellison, and First Class Petty Officer Brice Johnson climbed aboard the LST, followed by Matt Diamond and Jason Marks. The rest of the SEAL platoon stayed on *Mighty Mo*. These men got together with Abrams, Romanski, Soto, Bagley, and Lieutenant Commander Harker of the Seawolves to plan the operation for that night.

The SEAL platoon would go in under cover of darkness, just before sunup, and check out the area the Seawolf team had discovered the night before. They wanted to find out the damage the Seawolves had done and if the encounter had any connection to the flow of arms off the island to the VC troops in the rest of the Delta region. It was already known that Doung Island was the main source of supplies to the famous Zigzag Treeline area as well as the rest of the Delta. What wasn't known was how the VC were doing it. If the SEALs were lucky, they'd get a prisoner or two out of the operation and get some answers to their questions.

Once the plan was set, everyone hit his bed early.

They wanted to be fully rested when it was time to move out on the operation. All clocks were set for a wake-up call at 0200 hours. That would give the team time to put on their makeup and their combat gear and take the MSSC to the insertion point.

After nightfall, the Special Boat Squadron personnel that operated *Mighty Mo* cast off all lines to the LST and got under way as the SEAL Team slept. They were headed for a point in the middle of the Bassac River that would be closer to the area in question. That would be the most accessible place for insertion and extraction of the team. Once there, the anchor was dropped and they sat dead still in the river, completely blacked out. They wanted to keep *Mighty Mo* invisible to anyone on shore. Meanwhile, the Special Boat Squadron sailors stayed on full alert, manning all the guns until it was time for their SEAL buddies to wake up. It was going to be a long night.

Finally, 0200 hours arrived. Quietly, the men got up and prepared for the mission at hand. All of them put on tiger-striped fatigues.

Stuart Joynt had a tiger-striped floppy hat on. His weapon of choice was a Stoner—a belt-fed M-16 with a drum attached under the gun like the old tommy gun of gangster fame except it held 100 rounds. He had 800 rounds of belted 5.56 ammunition crisscrossing his chest and around his waist. On his web gear there were six V-40 grenades, one concussion grenade, one gas grenade, and two pop flares. A K-bar knife was taped to his shoulder, and a directional flashlight with a red lens was attached to his other shoulder. On his belt, besides his canteen of water, he had a first aid pouch and one red smoke grenade.

Brent "Animal" Ellison had cut the arms out of his

fatigue top, exposing huge biceps and triceps. His pants were a little high water and on his feet were his usual high-top tennis shoes. His bald head, face, and arms were completely covered in dark green, light green, and black makeup that had been applied with the skill of the highest paid makeup artist in Hollywood. The rest of the group only had it on their faces, since the sleeves of their tiger-striped shirts covered their arms.

Animal Ellison's weapon of choice was a CAR-15—a stumpy-looking M-16. He had one 50-round magazine inserted in his gun, with two other 50-round magazines taped to the bottom half of that clip. Six more 50-round magazines were attached to the front of his web gear, which he wore like a vest. Under his left armpit, in a shoulder holster, was a Smith & Wesson model 22 with a silencer. A K-bar knife was taped to his left shoulder, and on the other shoulder, like Joynt, he had a directional flashlight with a red lens. The rest of his web gear contained four frag grenades, two smoke grenades, two pop flares, and a first aid pouch. On his back was a Starlight Scope hung on a sling.

The other SEALs were similarly armed, with some variations. Brice "Outlaw" Johnson had an M-60 machine gun with 400 rounds of 7.62 strapped across his chest and a LAAW rocket slung over his shoulder. Matt "Big Daddy" Diamond, in a floppy tiger-striped hat, was armed with an M-203, which is an M-16 with an M-79 grenade launcher mounted underneath. He had magazines taped together onto the gun and to the front of his web gear vest; grenades around his waist, with a first aid pouch and canteen of water; a LAAW rocket on his back; and on his left shoulder, a

Gerber Mk-1 knife; the same directional flashlight the other men had; and a Smith & Wesson model 22 with a silencer.

The radioman, Jason "Goat" Marks, had a torn-up olive drab T-shirt covering his head and tied in the back, making him look like a pirate. On his back was the PRC-25 radio. Elsewhere on his body, he was armed to the teeth with bullets, grenades, and weapons.

Chris Holland had an M-60 with his 400 rounds of .308 strapped around his waist and chest, as well as grenades and a LAAW rocket slung over his back. Mike "Mikey" Collier wore a torn-up olive drab T-shirt on his head, like Goat Marks, and carried a Stoner, with 800 rounds, grenades, two pop flares, a K-bar knife; he also had a LAAW rocket slung on his back.

Robert "Doc" Stinehour was the medic. Besides all his medical supplies, he carried a Stoner and 800 rounds. Brad Mitchell had an M-203, magazines, six M-79 grenades, a knife, and a LAAW rocket.

The last member of the group, an LDNN—Lien Doc Nguoi Nhia, or "soldier who fights under the sea"—was a Vietnamese SEAL known merely as Ben. He carried an M-16 with three 50-round magazines taped together along with the standard vest with six more magazines. The other stuff he had was basically the same as the others', except he wasn't carrying a LAAW rocket.

All of the SEALs also had their black inflatable life vests on under their other stuff.

It was time to head out. The heavily armed group went over the side of *Mighty Mo* and into the very fast MSSC. Surrounding the radar tower in the middle and taking seats on the floor, the squad got as comfortable as possible for the ride to the insertion point. Sitting with their legs crossed, they resembled a group of Indians.

Special Boat Squadron sailor Ron Spears, from Mississippi, was at the wheel up front—five feet ten inches tall and a solid 170 pounds of muscle. Steve Madison, from Wisconsin, was the other Special Boat Squadron person on board. He manned one of the M-60s in case the boat got hit on their way out after they dropped off the SEALs. With their tiger-striped fatigues and floppy hats, the sailors blended right in with the SEALs on board.

Spears cranked up the two big block V8s. They could hardly be heard, because of the foam wrapped around the engine compartment. But they could be felt. The two Jacuzzi jet pumps came alive as Spears pushed the craft into gear. Madison cast off the bow and stern lines. Easing the throttles forward, the boat moved slowly away from the *Mighty Mo,* then Spears pushed the throttles to the maximum position and they skimmed across the surface of the river with ease.

Spears had been briefed on the route the SEALs were to take and where the dropoff point was located. At the speed they were traveling, it didn't take long to get to the target canal on Doung Island.

Approaching the edge of the island, Spears cut back on the power about halfway. He could see the mouth of the canal on his radarscope, and once it was visible to the naked eye, he stopped using the scope as a guide. Madison was watching intently as he kept a firm grip on one of the forward M-60s, ready to rock and roll.

Sliding up the little creek, every eye scanned both banks for some sign of trouble. All weapons were at the ready. If the tension had been any higher, they could have built a tree house in it.

At about fifteen knots, it wouldn't take long to get to the insertion point. Spears had to steer carefully as he followed the winding canal, sliding the MSSC this way and that. He worked the boat like an Olympic figure skater performing smooth, gliding moves across the ice.

Spears was thinking, The fork in this canal should be coming up any second now. Don't forget. Let them off on the left side of the left fork. Okay, boys, there she is.

Pointing the boat at the spot his passengers were supposed to get off, he pulled back all the way on the throttles and let the craft slide, without making a sound, into the muddy bank.

The first man off was Animal Ellison, the platoon point man. The reason he exposed as much skin as possible was because he believed he could feel the jungle better and be able to tell where booby traps or VC were hiding. As weird as that seemed to some, he got results, and sometimes those results were so strange that he might have actually felt something out there.

Next in line was Outlaw Johnson with his M-60. He followed Animal's footsteps as closely as possible, to disguise their number in case someone came across their tracks, and also to keep from hitting a booby trap. They stayed as far as they could from each other while still keeping in sight, to communicate.

Stuart Joynt climbed out of the MSSC next with his Stoner, followed by Goat Marks with the radio and his M-203, then Doc Stinehour with his Stoner, Ben the Vietnamese SEAL with his M-16, Brad Mitchell with his M-203, Mikey Collier with his Stoner, Big

Daddy Diamond with his M-203, and the rear guard Chris with his M-60.

No sooner had each one hit the jungle than he became invisible to Spears, who knew it was time to get away. He reversed the jet on one of the Jacuzzi pumps, hit the throttles to full power, and spun the boat like a top. Pointing her out the same way she had come in, he put both pumps in the same direction, and sped off.

The MSSC, light as a feather, moved like greased lightning down that canal, sliding its rear end this way and that as Spears maneuvered the boat down through the winding waterway. As he straightened her out one way, he had to immediately turn the steering wheel in the other direction, slipping the boat in a sideways motion around the next corner, back and forth, to the left and then back to the right, spraying water up on the muddy bank. Moving straight for a little bit and then another hard left, Spears was one with the boat, as Madison, gripping his machine gun, kept his eyes peeled for anything that might signal an ambush. Moments later, with complete silence, the Medium Seal Support Craft ejected itself from the Doung Island canal and was free once again in the Bassac River.

14

Animal Ellison was thinking that, as far back as he could remember, his parents raised him with a stern hand. They were very fair, but stern. He couldn't ever get away with anything. His father always seemed to know what he was doing, without Animal telling him as much, as if he had a sixth sense. Sometimes he'd let Animal get away with something, but would tell him that he knew and was giving him a break this time. At any rate, Animal believed that he inherited his ability to see things way before anyone else did from his father. Just like his father knew what he was doing as a child. People thought he was weird that way, but it was okay with Animal. He never cared what people thought of him anyway.

Animal had begun lifting weights when he was young, and also got into martial arts. While other parents were giving their kids piano lessons or guitar lessons or dance, his parents were paying for the martial arts classes. He hated going to those, but they paid off as he got older. Also, he never had any peer pressure, because most kids were scared of him.

He loved contact sports, football in particular. He was a linebacker, hit harder than anyone else on the field, and was offered a full scholarship to the University of Texas, but turned it down to join the Navy. Besides loving football, he loved the water. The one thing he never got to do was scuba dive, though it had intrigued him ever since he saw a movie about Navy frogmen with James Garner. I have to do that! he thought. He couldn't get it out of his mind.

But now, instead of diving under German ships and blowing them up, he was in South Vietnam, sneaking through thick jungle on his hands and knees, being bit by every kind of bug he could think of and some he couldn't, looking for anything that drew his attention. It wasn't his idea of fun, but what might be at the end of this excursion into the jungle would definitely be his idea of fun. There were some serious contact sports up ahead, except after he tackled them, he could kill them.

The jungle was extremely thick as Animal moved forward, watching, listening, and feeling in his own special way for booby traps or VC. His CAR-15 was in his right hand with the safety off and the selector switch on full automatic. In his left hand he held a long blade of grass that he moved up and down in front of him, looking for trip wires. He advanced through the undergrowth with his left foot forward and on his right knee, then slid up on his left knee, his right foot moving forward. With his large frame, he left a comfortable-size area for those following in his steps to get through safely.

Being the strange egg that he was, Animal felt no stress. With his intuition feelers out, he kept moving forward. Since he had long legs and sometimes way too much confidence in his ability, the pace he set was going to make the estimated time of arrival earlier than anticipated. He was thinking, Man, this is great. No booby traps at all. I sure hope this keeps up.

Outlaw was moving easily behind Animal, given the large safety space in the jungle Animal was leaving for the team. Standing in a half squat, Outlaw moved through the undergrowth with his M-60 at the ready, watching the area to the left of Animal for any sign of movement that would signal a possible ambush.

The LT, Joynt, with his Stoner at the ready, was behind Outlaw, watching to the right. As Joynt pushed through the jungle, it closed behind him and was then pushed open again as Goat came through with his M-203 pointing to the left. The incredible variety of leaves and branches slid over and past the PRC-25 on the radioman's back, closing again on the path behind him. The brush was opened again as Doc moved through, his Stoner pointed to the right. The little Vietnamese SEAL, Ben, followed, his M-16 pointing left. Then Mitchell parted the greenery with his body, his M-203 pointing to the right. As the leaves slid past the LAAW rocket on his back and closed once again over the path that was now being made, Mikey pushed through, his Stoner pointing to the left. He had added a nice piece of equipment that he'd picked up just before leaving the boat—a large satchel charge. He'd had a feeling they might need it before the operation was over. Following Mikey was Big Daddy, his M-203 covering the right. The last man, staying close behind Big Daddy, was Holland, his M-60 covering 180 degrees behind them. The reason he stayed so close to Big Daddy was because he had to walk backward and didn't want to lose his way.

Hey, this is interesting, Animal thought. A path in the woods, and it's straight too. That meant it was a human path, not an animal path. Animal paths always moved in a zigzag fashion. He thought: We need to look extra close for traps along here.

He decided to stay off the path and not cross over. It was going in the direction the team had to go anyway. He'd just keep the guys in the jungle, with his eye on the path as they moved parallel to it. Passing the signal back to Outlaw about what was up front and what he would do, Animal got the message relayed to the entire group.

From here on he knew he would have to be extra careful. Working his strand of grass and paying attention to his sixth sense, he moved forward with even more caution.

It wasn't long before all ten men had moved past the point at which Animal had first seen the evidence of a path through the jungle. Then Animal saw something else on the jungle floor in front of him: a human hand, or rather, a piece of a human hand. Two fingers and part of the palm were missing. Passing the information on to Outlaw, he moved on.

Then he came upon a foot. He knew that Charlie usually cleaned up after himself, so he assumed that the VC had missed a couple of pieces. Animal looked around the area in front of him and noticed evidence of an explosion. Clearly, this was where one of the Seawolf rockets had hit.

He moved on, making his way past that explosion site and coming upon another one. Continuing on past that spot, he found still another one. Damn, Seawolf, you blew the shit out of these guys, he thought. As he kept moving, he found tiny bits and pieces of body parts. Perhaps only Animal could have discovered them under all the leaves on the floor of the jungle.

Suddenly, every muscle in his body froze. Instantly, he became part of the jungle around him. Outlaw followed suit, as did the rest of the team on down the line. Animal's past experience coupled with his incredible intuitiveness told him something was just ahead of them. His eyes didn't move, or even blink. He just stared straight ahead. Using his left hand with the blade of grass in it, he very slowly moved his Starlight Scope around from his back. Keeping his right hand on his CAR-15 at the ready, he maneuvered the scope up to his left eye. Peering through it, he could see clearly just past the jungle in front of him to a clearing with trees. They were banana trees. Damn, he thought, there's a banana plantation straight in front of us. He passed the information back down the line.

Hanging the scope down to his left side, he continued forward, but extremely slowly, like a spaceman on another planet in the movies moving in slow motion. Outlaw gave him a little more space before he started moving up behind him.

As Animal reached the edge of the clearing, he became part of the jungle again, peering past the leaves with the Starlight Scope. Scanning from left to right, he saw that the orchard was clear of heat registration, which would have shown up if there was a person out there.

As he got all the way around to the right of the clearing in his scan, he stopped abruptly. He'd spotted Charlie, his scope lighting up with a heat registration. Animal kept the scope on him and tried to see past the VC. It looked like there was something else out there,

Top: Navy Combat Aircrew
Wings
Middle: Navy Aircrew
Wings
Bottom: Navy Pilot Wings
(Author's collection)

Helicopter in flight close to palm trees in background.
(Courtesy of U.S. Navy through Lyle Nimmo)

Helicopter in flight, with rocket being discharged. (Courtesy of U.S. Navy through Lyle Nimmo)

Where the crew chief sits—in the back. Note the 2,000-round door box for his M-60 machine gun. Also the pussy pole with the smoke grenade attached to it. The flex gun ammo boxes are on the floor next to the crew chief's seat. His helmet is hanging on the wall above the seat. The Mae West and armor vest are sitting on the seat. (Courtesy of Steve McAllister)

The front office of a Huey. The backs of the pilot and copilot seats hold extra M-60 barrels, parts, M-79 grenade launchers, and M-16s. You can also see the asbestos gloves that were used to change the hot barrels. (Courtesy of Steve McAllister)

Daniel Kelly and Steve McAllister. (Courtesy of Steve McAllister)

John Luscher and Jack Bolton the morning after the Tet Offensive. (Courtesy of Fred Record)

Ray Robinson lost his life on Doung Island. (Courtesy of Fred Record)

John Luscher after kicking ass in Saigon. (Courtesy of John Luscher)

Captain Spencer, our leader and our friend. (Courtesy of Captain Spencer)

Freddy "Buddy" Record (Courtesy of Fred Record)

Lyle Nimmo taking a break in the Seawolf compartment on board the LST while up the river. (Courtesy of Lyle Nimmo)

Fred "Buddy" Record. Ready to depart on the next mission. Note the rocket pod and M-60 machine guns on the pylon. (Courtesy of Fred Record)

Chuck Bagley. He always had a great attitude. (Courtesy of Fred Record)

Lt. Octavio Soto feeling very good about himself. (Courtesy of Fred Record)

Celebrating the 3,000th landing on the *Harnett County*. Front row: unknown, Chuck Bagley, John Abrams, and Mike Hammergren. Back row: Dave Cranor, Octavio Soto, and Les Wantz. John Abrams lost his life on Doung Island. (Courtesy of Fred Record)

John Abrams's helicopter after they retrieved it from Doung Island. (Courtesy of Fred Record)

Doung Island where Abrams's bird went down. (Courtesy of Fred Record)

a very large hooch that was probably the main farm-house. It seemed there was activity behind the house, and he decided to get a better look at it.

Animal passed the information back to Outlaw, who in turn passed it back to Joynt. The LT decided to take a look for himself, and slowly moved up past Outlaw. Communicating through hand signals, Joynt made the decision to take out the VC closest to them so the team could move in for a closer look at what was going on behind the main hooch.

Moving his Starlight Scope to his back, Animal be-gan to move in on his prey. He was like a cat as he took each step in the jungle with slow, deliberate mo-tions, stopping every couple of seconds in a totally frozen position. The CAR-15 seemed to levitate to his left hand. Then, with his right hand, he pulled his si-lenced Smith & Wesson from its shoulder holster un-der his left armpit. He was almost to the point in the jungle line adjacent to the unaware VC, who stood with an AK-47 slung over his shoulder, wearing the typical black VC pajamas. Animal's intended victim was about ten paces from the jungle line, seemingly not expecting a thing. Joynt had shadowed his point man all the way, ready to retrieve the body as soon as it was immobilized. Animal took careful aim and slowly squeezed the trigger. There was a little pop, and then the projectile hit its mark square in the man's temple, dropping him like a wet rag.

Joynt moved from the jungle edge, grabbed the VC by his shirt, and dragged him back into the jungle. This all occurred in little more than an eye blink. The LT, who was as large and as strong as Animal, made it a simple task making the body disappear in rapid fashion.

The LT passed the VC's AK-47 back down the line to Ben. Our Vietnamese SEAL slung the weapon over his shoulder as the group continued to move down the edge of the jungle to get a better position on the activity still going on behind the main hooch.

Animal stopped abruptly again. It appeared to him that they'd come to the far canal that led back out to their extraction point. It was the same one that ran directly behind the big hooch. He motioned for the LT to come forward once again.

The location of the canal needed to be confirmed with Joynt, who pulled out his map and checked it using his red-lensed flashlight. Sure enough, it was the same canal.

Once that was done, they turned their attention to the VC they could now clearly see behind the big hooch. The sun hadn't come up yet, but they could tell that it would soon. The sky had lightened considerably.

After careful examination of this new target using the Starlight Scope, Joynt went back to his original position and passed the word to make a skirmish line in preparation to take out the excellent target of opportunity.

What they were looking at was about twenty VC loading a large sampan with weapons and several B-40 rockets. There were four more in the sampan wrapping the arms in banana leaves and staking bananas on top of them. One large sampan had already been loaded and was starting to move. It wasn't going any faster than a bass boat with the trolling motor going, and was moving toward the SEALs to go out the canal that would lead to the south Bassac River and over to the Zigzag Treeline. Sitting in the middle of that river was *Mighty Mo,* waiting to send the MSSC in to extract the SEALs when the mission was over.

Joynt, Animal, Outlaw, and the rest knew they didn't have much time. Things were about to accelerate into overdrive any second. The word was passed quickly. Big Daddy and Mikey would send their two LAAW rockets into the main farmhouse—the big hooch with a thatched roof on it—to kill or scare any other troops out of there. Joynt and Outlaw would send their two LAAW rockets into the approaching sampan. Mitchell would send his LAAW rocket into the sampan that was still being loaded. Goat would pop his M-79 grenade out of his M-203 at the same sampan that Mitchell was hitting. Animal would be blasting any survivors on the approaching sampan that the two LAAW rockets didn't kill. Doc would be concentrating his Stoner on the twenty personnel behind the farmhouse. Ben's M-16 would also be killing VC behind the farmhouse. Holland and his M-60 would be literally blowing body parts off VC behind the farmhouse.

When all the LAAW rockets had been fired, they would be discarded, and then the men would start firing their main weapons. Mitchell and Big Daddy would pop their M-79 grenades at the sampan still being loaded, then start firing their M-203s on full automatic, along with all the others.

The signal for everyone to start shooting would come from Joynt, when he fired his LAAW. Once the rockets had gone off, everyone would move from the jungle in a straight line, walking toward the VC with their guns up, taking aim and shooting at the same time.

The sun still hadn't quite come up, but it was close

enough now so everyone could see very well. Joynt took aim at the approaching sampan and pushed the go button. The LAAW rocket made its usual incredibly loud exploding sound as it left the tube. On top of that, four went off at the same time. A split second later, three M-79 grenades found their mark, exploding body parts everywhere.

The team burst from the jungle line as the farmhouse burst into flames from the rockets' explosions. The VC on the dock out back were frozen with surprise and sheer terror from seeing the men with the green faces coming out of the jungle. A few of them reached for their weapons, but were blown full of holes before they could use them.

The sampan that was already under way lost two of its occupants to the exploding LAAW rockets. The other two on board were killed instantly by Animal's CAR-15 sending thirty rounds of 5.56 tearing through their torsos. The sampan was starting to sink as it aimlessly drifted into the bank.

Outlaw had turned his attention to the other boat and was working it over with his M-60. As the .308s hit the canal, water shot up eight feet into the air. When they hit the boat, wood chips exploded, leaving large holes. One of the VC on the sampan grabbed his AK-47 and took aim at the SEALs. Outlaw's M-60 blew one of his arms off and put a round in his head, which exploded like a watermelon. Joynt, meanwhile, was spraying down the dock with his Stoner, killing VC. Their bodies jumped as his 5.56 rounds found their marks. Goat was also cleaning up the dock with his M-203. Doc Stinehour was doing his part with his Stoner. Ben was changing magazines and then continuing to fire his M-16. Mitchell had turned his attention and his M-203 to the VC coming out of the burning house with AK-47s in their hands. Mikey had done the same with his Stoner. Big Daddy's M-203 had reloaded and was also getting in on the party coming out of the house. As the VC came out the door they were being cut to ribbons by the bullets from the SEALs. Holland had hooked up another belt in his M-60 and was now cutting people in half again. By this time the SEALs had traveled over half the distance from the jungle to the back of the house.

A moment later all was quiet. The strong smell of gunpowder hung over the banana plantation as the team moved in on the massacre sight. And it was indeed a massacre. It appeared that the VC hadn't gotten off one shot.

Those who needed to reload did so while the others covered them. Moving in to check for survivors, everyone kept their guns up, aiming at anything that might pose a threat. Mikey, Big Daddy, and Holland tossed some more grenades into the house, then entered it, clearing a room at a time. Animal, Goat, Doc, Ben, and Mitchell set up a perimeter, while Outlaw and Joynt looked over the boatload of weapons.

Mikey, Big Daddy, and Holland surfaced from the house with a prisoner who was untouched. Outstanding! the men thought. All this good stuff and a prisoner too! It didn't get any better than that.

Without Joynt saying a word to anyone, the men instinctively knew it was time to get the hell out of Dodge. After all, they had been making an awful lot of noise. If there were any more VC anywhere on the island, they would all be headed this way.

Mikey, Big Daddy, and Holland had the prisoner handcuffed and blindfolded. They turned him over to

Joynt and Goat, then grabbed some weapons from the damaged sampan that still sat at the dock behind the house. Holland motioned to Animal, Doc, Ben, and Mitchell that he, Big Daddy, and Mikey would watch the perimeter while they got their share of captured weapons from the boat. Outlaw had already grabbed a B-40 rocket and an AK-47.

Animal took the lead, as usual. Outlaw fell in behind him. Joynt and Goat had the prisoner in tow. Doc, Ben, and Mitchell were moving right behind them. Mikey and Big Daddy slowly backed out of the perimeter and followed the others up the canal. Holland, walking backward with his M-60 pointed to the rear, moved as quickly as he could without tripping.

The Special Boat Squadron guys had not been briefed to come down the canal this far to pick them up. The SEAL Team was going to have to move about one klick up the canal before they'd reach the specified extraction point.

Mikey was looking at the sampan that had been on its way out when they hit it. It sat half sunk and up against the bank on the canal.

That's why he'd brought that satchel charge along, he realized. Now he could blow the living shit out of the boat so they didn't have to try and dig all the weapons out of the mud and pack them up along with the ones they already had.

Animal had come up even with the half-sunken sampan when he got one of his funny feelings again, the kind his dad used to have. His sixth sense was going nuts. He froze in his footsteps as if about to step on a mine. Outlaw stopped when he saw Animal stop, and so on all the way back to Chris. Animal turned around slowly and looked back at Holland, then gazed off in the distance toward the far side of the plantation at the treeline.

"Boys," Animal said, "we are about to jump square into a shit storm! Let's move!"

And with that said—*crack! crack! crack! crack!*— several hundred AK-47 rounds came whizzing past them, accompanied by green tracers. They were all coming out of the jungle Animal was looking at. He saw muzzle flashes that looked like a thousand firecrackers going off. The enemy fire hit Holland and Mitchell. One round had slashed through the fleshy part of Holland's left shoulder and another round grazed his right upper leg, not hitting anything vital. He dropped to one knee as he opened up with his M-60, spraying the jungle beyond the house. Mitchell felt a sting in his side as one just scratched him. He had already turned around and was shooting an M-79 grenade in the direction of the fire.

Animal knew that the jungle edge they were heading for was still too far away for them to escape any more injuries. The muddy bank of the canal was the only choice they had to duck for cover. Holland's and Mitchell's wounds had to be taken care of before they tried to move into the protection of the jungle.

Big Daddy and Mikey happened to be carrying captured B-40 rockets. As they slid into the canal's edge they sent the rockets at the VC in the far treeline. As the rockets exploded in the jungle, the rest of the team got into a defensive position, prepared for anything.

15

Doc was tending to Chris Holland's wounds first. Mitchell wasn't waiting. He just patched himself up while lying in the mud on the bank just below the line of fire. The rest of the SEALs were occasionally returning short bursts to let Charlie know they weren't going to just sit there and take any shit.

Luckily, they had a load of captured AK-47s with them, as well as several B-40 rockets that were left. And they still had plenty of ammo for their personal weapons.

Using the half-sunk sampan as cover, the team got in their usual back-to-back circle position. This kept them protected on all sides. As soon as Chris was moved into their defensive posture, muzzle flashes from the VC popped up from the jungle just down and across the canal. It was not looking good for the SEAL hunters and killers.

LT Joynt grabbed the phone off the PRC-25 radio on Goat's back. Keying the mike, he said, "Iron Hat, Scorpion One. I say again, Iron Hat, Scorpion One. Scramble Seawolf. Scramble Seawolf. Over." A moment of silence. Then, "Scorpion One, Scorpion One. Iron Hat. Seawolf en route. Over."

It was music to Joynt's ears. "Iron Hat, Scorpion One," he said. "I copy. Also get medevac en route to your location. We have two WIAs [wounded in action]. Over."

"Roger, Scorpion One. Will do."

Back at the LST, Soto was sitting in his chopper when the alarm sounded. Nimmo and Buddy had just finished the morning's preflight inspection. Bagley came running out to the flight deck with Romanski right on his heels. Abrams, Wobbe, and Robbie were sitting in their aircraft, taking a break from their morning's work. With everyone sitting there, waiting for a scramble that could come at any moment, both birds got off the deck in record-breaking time.

Soto was already turning his gunship up when Bagley jumped in the copilot's seat. Nimmo and Buddy had put the rocket contacts down and locked the flex gun barrels in and were already sitting in their positions, guns in their laps and helmets on. Wobbe was out in front of their chopper, holding down the rotor blade. Robbie had put their rocket contacts down, locked in the flex gun barrels, and was in position with his helmet on. Abrams was double-checking the coordinates of the SEAL Team location.

As Soto and his guys pulled up into a hover, Romanski was getting strapped into his copilot seat. Soto transmitted over the radio that was set on the team's PRC-25 frequency, "Seawolf One-four is off at this time." And over the side they went, first dipping down toward the water, then slowly coming back up as they gained speed.

Abrams immediately turned up his jet engine. The main rotor blade was pulled from Wobbe's hands. Robbie was in position, ready to go kick some VC ass. Wobbe ran around and jumped in his seat. Robbie hit his ICS and said, "We're clear, sir!"

"Roger!" Abrams said.

Up and over the side of the ship they went, with Abrams saying on his radio, "Seawolf One-five is off at this time!"

Soto was already streaking downriver at low level. Abrams was pushing his bird to the limits, trying to catch up.

LT Joynt, Outlaw, and the rest were ducking behind the half-sunk sampan, firing like crazy at the two VC positions. Doc had finished with Chris and was taking a look at Mitchell. Despite his wounds, Chris was busily shooting his M-60. Mitchell waved off Doc, saying he was fine, so Doc turned around and started doing his thing with his Stoner.

As Ben and Outlaw launched their B-40 rockets into the treeline across the canal from them, they heard the popping sound of approaching helicopters in the distance. In between shooting three-round bursts at the enemy's position, Animal was thinking about how fast the Seawolves had responded. It seemed they'd called the Seawolves just three or four minutes ago.

The Special Boat Squadron guys had already dispatched the MSSC to the pickup location. Besides Ron Spears and Steve Madison, a third man had joined them in the boat—Vernon Barber, originally from Trinidad. He had a musical accent and was built like an Olympic athlete. Barber had once played professional soccer, stood about five feet eight inches tall, and was a born killer.

Over the radio, Joynt heard: "Scorpion One, Seawolf One-four. Where do ya want it? Over."

The LT stopped shooting and grabbed the phone off Goat's back. "We're popping red smoke. Hit the treeline to the north of the banana plantation, and if you can see the canal, we need you to hit the treeline on the east side of that. As soon as you hit 'em, we're moving straight south to our pickup point. Over."

"Roger, Scorpion One. We're rolling in at this time," Soto answered.

Animal pulled the pin on his red smoke grenade and tossed it out on the ground next to the muddy bank where they were.

Soto was starting his run just as Abrams fell in on his six o'clock position. Soto hit the radio button on his stick and said, "I have red smoke, Scorpion One."

That was confirming to the SEAL Team on the ground that everything was straight on their location.

Soto continued, "Seawolf One-five, One-four. Put two darts on the edge of the canal and two darts on the far treeline. Break left."

"Roger, One-four. Two darts on canal's edge and two darts on far treeline with a left break," came back over the radio.

Soto started his run at 800 feet. Bagley opened up with the flex guns and concentrated on the far treeline. Nimmo was hitting the far treeline with his M-60, and Buddy was strafing the treeline along the canal. The

Seawolf team was coming right over the top of the SEALs' position. Soto punched off two rockets. The sparks flew as they cleared the tubes. He then adjusted the angle of the chopper and punched off two more rockets that sailed toward the far treeline. He broke off at 400 feet to clear the area for Abrams.

Joynt didn't have to say anything to his guys because of the times they'd operated under these very same conditions. Soto's rockets buzzed over their heads and crashed into the jungle next to the canal, exploding with such force that the SEALs could feel the shock wave go right through them. Then they all started their leapfrog move toward the jungle's edge, leading south down the canal. Outlaw changed places with Chris, because of Chris's wounds.

As Animal started toward the jungle, brass from the six M-60 machine guns being fired on the Seawolf chopper overhead rained down on the SEALs like a cloudburst in the middle of a monsoon. Joynt, with his Stoner, was firing like crazy to cover Animal's retreat. Once the point man had reached the treeline, he turned and fired to cover Joynt and Goat, who were running as well as they could while dragging the prisoner.

The SEAL Team was laying down some serious fire, with M-60s, M-203s, and Stoners, the brass ejected from their guns splashing into the canal. Ben and Mitchell moved around Chris and Doc, getting ready to cover their retreat. Mikey, Big Daddy, and Outlaw were getting ready to cut loose next.

Soto's third and fourth rockets hit the far treeline right on target. The men on the ground heard the terrifying sound of the gunships as they came overhead, placing the strike. The sound of the rockets was enough to turn their blood ice cold.

Mikey, Big Daddy, and Outlaw, completely reloaded, were ready for Chris and Doc to make their move. Doc grabbed Chris's arm and they headed for the jungle. Ben, Mitchell, Mikey, Big Daddy, and Outlaw opened up. Joynt, Animal, and Goat did the same from the treeline by the canal. Two more rockets hit the enemy positions closest to the SEALs. Then two more blasted into the far treeline. Another shower of brass came down as the second Seawolf chopper passed overhead.

That was the cue for the last men in the team to move. Outlaw, Ben, Mitchell, Mikey, and Big Daddy headed out for the treeline next to the canal that led to the rendezvous point. Animal, Joynt, Goat, Doc, and Chris opened up from the jungle with all they had, blasting the hell out of the two treelines.

Their prisoner, with his hands tied behind his back and blindfolded, was lying on the ground, with Joynt's and Goat's feet planted on him.

As Mikey passed the half-sunk sampan, he tossed his satchel charge in it with the timer already set. Hopefully, it would give the pursuing VC time to get up next to it before it went off.

By now, everyone was in the jungle and the Seawolves were coming in with a second run.

"One-five, One-four, two and two, same as before. Break right."

"Roger, One-four. Same as before with right-hand break."

This time brass from the choppers didn't rain on the SEALs because they were coming in from a different direction. *Blam, blam, blam, blam.* Four more rockets exploded on the enemy's positions. It was a mixture of high explosive and white phosphorus warheads. The WP were the ones that set a person on fire and couldn't be put out.

Nimmo, Buddy, Robbie, and Wobbe had spotted the VC running through the plantation toward the SEALs. Now they were taking them out with their machine guns.

As Outlaw shot back at the enemy, he could see them trying to make it across the plantation. Four M-60s from the gunners above were exploding VC heads and tearing arms and legs off. The .308s were kicking up dirt and chopping hunks of banana tree all over the place.

The SEALs under the cover of jungle started their leapfrog again. Outlaw, at rearguard, noticed that the VC were moving along with them on the other side of the canal, and were gaining. That wasn't good. He kept firing his M-60 at the muzzle flashes in the jungle until it was time for him to move.

Big Daddy yelled at Outlaw that it was his turn to go, then popped an M-79 across the canal and followed up with a full clip on full automatic as Outlaw passed him. While he was shooting, he also noticed that the VC from the far treeline were moving across the plantation, charging toward them. There were so many, he couldn't count them all. However, he also noticed that the Seawolves above were slowing the VC down.

Mikey cut loose with his Stoner, and Big Daddy moved. When it was Doc's turn to lay down cover fire, he was met with a shock wave that was an eye opener and an ear closer: Mikey's satchel charge went off in the sampan.

"One-five, One-four. Did you see that explosion? Over."

"Roger!" Abrams said.

The Seawolves were in the middle of their third strike when Mikey's little treat went off. Soto and Abrams thought they had set off a secondary explosion. It wasn't until later, at the debriefing, that they found out what it really was. The explosion was so big, it blew some of the VC off the bank and back into the jungle. It also effectively cleared out a bunch who were charging across the banana plantation.

The combination of the Seawolves' rockets and machine-gun fire coupled with Mikey's satchel charge slowed the main force of VC long enough for the SEAL Team to make headway toward their rendezvous point.

Madison and Barber, with Spears at the controls, were flying across the Bassac River in their MSSC, heading for the far canal to pick up the SEAL Team. The two gunners jacked back the charging handles on their M-60s and took their positions. They were on each side of Spears, so both sides of the canal could be covered once they entered into Doung Island.

Spears had already studied his map and committed all the turns of the canal to memory. That way he could take them very fast.

Steering a boat is not like driving a car. You have to think ahead. When you're going very fast in a narrow canal that winds this way and that, you have to commit to the turn early. That's because of the sliding factor. When you turn a speeding jet boat, the rear end slides out a bit before you actually make the turn.

Daniel E. Kelly

"All right, there it is, boys! Get ready!" Spears said.

"I'm ready!" Barber said.

"Me too!" Madison answered.

With that, the MSSC disappeared into the jungle of Doung Island and shot up the little canal.

16

Animal was sneaking along as fast as he could, looking for traps and any more VC that might have slipped by. He didn't want to bump into another firefight. The one he'd left behind was enough.

His teammates were still leapfrogging, with Joynt and Goat dragging their prisoner along. Animal was thinking, Keep working that leaf. Watch and feel for any clue to the location of any surprises. Come on, man, you can make it. He meanwhile took note of another Seawolf strike. He loved those guys, thought they had to be crazy, up there in the sky with nothing to hide behind. He preferred it down on the ground, where at least he had a lot of cover.

He knew he had to keep moving, with Joynt and Goat and the prisoner right behind him. He wondered how much farther it would be before he saw the boat. *Oh, shit!* There was movement up at his one o'clock position.

Animal signaled to Joynt that he had VC ahead. The platoon stopped leapfrogging and set up a defensive position. Animal moved up at his two o'clock position very slowly, attempting to get in behind whoever was there. On his hands and knees, he came up behind two VC. Was that all there was? he wondered. He decided to wait there a second to see if there was anyone else.

Joynt, the prisoner, and the rest were snuggled into the greenery around them. They couldn't be seen, but anyone who stumbled over them would be in trouble.

About a minute that seemed like an hour passed as Animal listened to the firefight going on behind him. Another VC showed up. All right, he thought, I'm glad I waited, but I can't wait any longer. As Joynt watched from his position, he saw Animal move in behind all three. They were obviously looking to ambush the SEALs. Moving in slower, Animal got up to about four feet from his target. They didn't expect that. They thought the SEALs would creep by in front of them, and that they'd pop holes in them.

All three VC had AK-47s with bandoleers of extra clips. They wore the typical black pajamas. Animal moved in, dropping his CAR-15 and grabbing the closest one around the neck with his left arm. He raised the man up and snapped his neck. At the same time, he gave the next closest one a karate chop to the brachial nerve of his neck, dropping him to the jungle floor without a sound. By now the third one had heard a sound from behind and turned around, only to come face-to-face with Animal's painted body. The unsuspecting VC, shocked and terrified at the same time, reflexively jumped straight up. Animal reached out, placing one hand on the VC's chin and the other hand to the back of his head. With a quick, jerking motion, as if he were opening a very large jar, he snapped the man's neck.

Afterward, Animal stood over two dead VC, with the third still unconscious. He heard something that sounded like people running through the jungle behind him. Grabbing one of the Charlies' AK-47s that lay at his feet, he spun around and cut loose with a burst, blowing two more VC backward into the jungle from whence they came.

Well, so much for being silent! Joynt could see where Animal was, and he decided to proceed on to the rendezvous point. Animal took up his spot after picking up his CAR-15 and taking his knife to the VC he'd knocked out. That made five dead VC plus more weapons that had to be picked up. The group passed the AK-47s down the line to make the load even. They were loaded down now with captured guns and rocket launchers, and hoping they wouldn't have much farther to go.

Animal began looking for more traps or more VC that might show up again as the leapfrogging continued. By now the VC on the far side of the canal had caught up with the SEALs. Plus, the SEALs were still getting fire from behind. Move and shoot. Move and shoot. That was the order of the day.

Animal hadn't found any more VC who were trying to cut them off from their extraction point. And then, to his relief, he peered out of the jungle's edge and saw the MSSC sliding up, almost hitting him in the nose with the front of the boat. He yelled at Joynt to come forward and get the prisoner loaded up.

As they moved past, Animal opened up on the far bank with his CAR-15. Once Joynt and Goat had gotten on board the boat, they opened up as well. Madison was shooting like crazy at the fire they were receiving from the other side of the canal. Barber had moved his M-60 over to that side as well and was also heating up his barrel with 7.62s.

Animal ran out of ammo. He popped his clip out

and slammed another one in. Chris, with Doc's help, had moved up next to Animal. They joined in and cut loose on the bank across from them. Mikey and Ben were shooting back behind them as they moved up next to Doc. Mitchell and Outlaw moved past and got in the boat. Empty brass ejected from all the guns was flying everywhere as the SEALs were shooting and at the same time boarding the MSSC.

Joynt had popped another red smoke grenade and had called for the Seawolves to put in a closer strike to their position. "Seawolf, can you hit the north and the east of my red smoke? Over."

"Roger that, Scorpion One. We're on it!" Soto said.

As Doc helped Chris into the boat, the SEALs could hear the eerie sound of the rotor blades as the Seawolves came diving down on their prey. Chris, getting settled in the boat, glanced down the canal in the direction they'd be going. What he saw shot a chill up his spine. It was the lead Seawolf chopper banking and twisting down the small creek at treetop level, coming straight at them. And the trail bird was jogging back and forth right behind.

"Jesus Christ!" he yelled.

The chopper had just punched off a rocket, and it looked like it was coming straight at them.

Chris yelled again, *"Duck, you mothers!"*

Swooooosh-bam! The rocket exploded in the jungle just off the bank across from the MSSC. Then they punched off another one. It hit right on the bank, but down a little farther. Two more were sent over their heads, so low they felt like they could jump up and catch them. They exploded in the jungle on their side back where the other VC were coming from. Like the other SEALs, Chris was gritting his teeth so hard, it felt to him like he'd flossed with a banjo string. Water was shooting up all around the boat as the flex guns and door gunners' M-60s made contact. The bank across from the boat and the jungle behind them was getting shredded, with all the .308s from above. The lead gunship flew just over the SEALs heads, with the skids on the chopper hitting the tops of the trees enough to send leaves falling all around the boat.

As that helicopter disappeared off to the right, the second Seawolf helicopter punched off two rockets that also looked like they were coming straight for the boat.

"Motherfucker! Here they come again!" Mitchell yelled.

The sound of rockets coming that close was terrifying. Those two also hit right where they were supposed to—on the bank in the jungle across from the SEALs.

Two more rockets went blasting by, headed for the jungle beyond where the team had come from. Meanwhile, tracers were flying by all around, coming from the approaching gunship. When the gunship screamed overhead, it knocked some of the treetops down in the canal, making the SEALs flinch and duck their heads.

"Holy shit, Stuart, ya think those bastards got any sense at all?" Chris yelled.

After a short pause, Joynt yelled over the gunfire, "I don't think so, thank God!"

With those explosions, Spears backed the boat off the mud bank, now that everyone was on board, and spun the boat around in the canal like a top. Getting pointed in the correct direction, he pushed the throttles balls to the wall. All guns on the boat were firing back into the jungle. The gunners on the two gunships were still tearing up the bank behind them. Spears was totally focused on the sharp turns in the canal as he maneuvered the MSSC around each bank and every S turn like the pro that he was. The boat was really moving. It occurred to him that, without all the bullets flying around, it would make a great ride that he could probably charge big bucks for.

By the time they reached the mouth of the canal and entered back onto the Bassac River, *Mighty Mo* had moved from its position down closer to where the MSSC was going to exit Doung Island. Once the Special Boat Squadron sailors had seen their teammates out in the river, they had coordinated with the Seawolves above and started laying down 81mm mortar fire and 106 recoilless rifle fire. The LST had weighed anchor and moved downriver as well. They also wanted to get in on the action with their 40mm cannon fire.

It had not been a good day for Charlie, Joynt thought to himself. The SEALs had two wounded, the prisoner was going to reveal something one way or the other, and Chris and Mitchell were getting a free ride back up to Binh Thuy in an Army medevac helicopter that was already waiting on the flight deck of the LST.

It had been another one of those "Thank you, Jesus" days.

17

Chris and Mitchell were enjoying a little R&R (rest and relaxation) up at the Binh Thuy Army Evac Hospital. They had cornered a couple of Army nurses, Lieutenants Lorraine Massie and Carolyn Galbraith. Lorraine was from Maryland, a five-foot-three-inch drop-dead-gorgeous redhead. Carolyn was a southern belle from Texas, five feet two inches tall, 110 pounds, and a brunette bombshell. The two SEALs laid on them the usual "I'm a poor wounded soldier who needs some personal tender loving care" routine, and the two smooth talkers were in high cotton.

Meanwhile, LT Joynt and the Vietnamese SEAL Ben were busy questioning their prisoner on *Mighty Mo*. Abrams, Soto, and the other Seawolves were back on the LST. Between the LST's big guns and *Mighty Mo*'s, there wasn't much left of the banana plantation or the jungle along the canal leading to it.

On *Mighty Mo*, Joynt and Ben weren't having much luck with their prisoner. However, Outlaw had an idea he thought would make Charlie more cooperative. It would take the assistance of the Seawolves to pull it off.

Joynt contacted Lieutenant Commander Harker and bounced the idea off him, and Harker found the idea very humorous and agreed to go along with the plan.

As a result, Joynt, Ben, Big Daddy, and Outlaw got Spears to transport them in the LSSC over to the LST with the prisoner. Once there, they climbed the ladder up to the flight deck, where Harker already had the two helicopters ready.

Soto, Bagley, Nimmo, and Buddy were going to be the lucky ones who would take their special cargo skyward. Abrams and his crew would fly cover.

Nimmo untied the rotor blade and walked it around front while Buddy locked in the flex gun barrels and put down the contacts on the rockets. Bagley climbed into his copilot seat and started the checklist with Soto, who was already strapped in. Buddy helped get Joynt and Ben situated on the flex gun ammo trays in the back with their prisoner, climbed in his door seat, put his helmet on, plugged into the ICS, and told Soto all was ready in the back.

Soto yelled out his door, "Clear! Coming hot!" And the jet engine slowly started to turn up. Poor Victor Charlie had no idea what was going on.

Abrams and his crew were all set. They just had to wait for Soto to lift off and clear the flight deck so they could start to turn up.

Big Daddy, Outlaw, and Spears shoved off from the LST and took their boat out into the middle of the river. Once Spears got them in position as close to the middle of the widest spot in the Bassac, he used the throttles to nurse the big 427s and Jacuzzi jet pumps to keep them as stationary as possible. Big Daddy and Outlaw, still dressed in their tiger-stripe fatigues and with their black inflatable vests on, lowered themselves over the side into the brown river water. They waited there, hanging on to the side of their boat.

By this time Soto and Seawolf 14 had taken off from the deck of the ship and started to climb to 1,000 feet. Abrams and his team were in the process of getting started.

Nimmo and Buddy were enjoying the show as Joynt and Ben were doing their thing. Ben had pulled a blindfold from his back pocket and was telling the VC that if he didn't cooperate and answer their questions, Joynt would throw him out of the helicopter. As Nimmo and Buddy looked on, it was evident that the prisoner wasn't buying it. So Joynt grabbed him and manhandled him over to the door in front of Nimmo. The prisoner's hands were tightly bound behind his back. Ben kept repeating himself as Joynt jerked him in and out of the wind in the doorway, making him look down at the jungle below. By this time Soto had them up to 1,000 feet over the land.

The LT brought the act to the next level. He grabbed the prisoner around the neck and hung him out the door, letting his feet dangle in space, then pulled him back in. Still no luck with the interrogation.

Joynt told Ben to put the blindfold on the VC. Once that was done, Nimmo got the high sign from the SEAL lieutenant and passed the word on to Soto via ICS. Soto said, "Roger that!"

Abrams, whose team had finally got up to speed and were behind Soto, had been briefed on what was going to happen. His team's job was to provide cover for his lead bird.

Soto started gradually down, so as not to raise suspicion. While he was doing that, Joynt kept yelling at the VC that he was going to toss him out. Of course, the prisoner now was unable to see what was going on.

It didn't take long for Soto to make his move from 1,000 feet over the land to 25 feet over the river. That's still very high. If you don't think so, look at an Olympic-size swimming pool with a 25-foot diving platform. Climb up and look down; it's a long way.

Soto edged over the top of Big Daddy and Outlaw, who were now out away from their boat, floating downriver with the current. The timing had to be just right or this poor Charlie could drown. The object was to get the information they needed, not kill him.

One last plea from Ben of his countryman to fess up the goods before the man with the green face tossed him to his doom. No luck! So out Charlie went.

As big as Joynt was, he had no problem tossing this poor soul out the door. He hit right on his back. *Splat!*

Big Daddy and Outlaw were right there to rescue him. It was a good thing too, because he was unconscious when they got to him. Outlaw held his head out of the water while Big Daddy revived him.

Spears jumped on the throttles of the LSSC and artfully slid it up next to the SEALs in the river. In a short while they had the prisoner on board and conscious again.

Later, back on the LST, the guys heard that the prisoner had suddenly become cooperative, that he'd spilled his guts.

Joynt told Nimmo to pass on to Soto via ICS that it would be nice if he could hover over the LSSC so he and Ben could jump out into the water and join their friends in the boat.

Soto agreed, and the SEALs jumped in. Again, it

was just moments before Spears had picked up those two.

The trick paid off. The prisoner told them all kinds of stuff. One important piece of information was that a big shipment would be coming in from the ocean, including a Chinese Communist .51 caliber machine gun. It was a gun that could shoot down F-4 Phantoms, not to mention helicopters. How it was coming in, the prisoner didn't know, but he knew someone who would. That someone was up in Binh Thuy. He said that he would show the SEALs where.

In the meantime, Joynt passed the valuable information on to the Coast Guard. They, in turn, set up a blockade just off Doung Island on the coast, using their fast cutters and the U.S. Navy swift boats. There was no way that gun was going to slip by.

Several days later Joynt and his band captured the head honcho up in Binh Thuy with the aid of their prisoner. After a typical SEAL Team interrogation, the head honcho told them there would be a sampan moving arms off the island, headed for the Zigzag Treeline, and that sampan would have the .51 caliber machine gun on board.

Damn it, Joynt thought. That damn gun is already here!

The VC informant went on to say it would be moved off Doung Island the following night.

The news spurred the SEAL Team into action. With Chris and Mitchell out of commission temporarily, Wayne "Tator" Hanson and Bob "Bullet" Crenshaw would be stepping in. Joynt also pulled Gary Stocker from his platoon to join them in going downriver.

Tator, from San Diego, got his nickname because he loved french fries. He also loved hot rods and racing. Bullet, from Ardmore, Oklahoma, got his call sign from the motorcycle racing circuit. Gary Stocker, an Oklahoma farm boy, loved guns and anything technical. He was an electrical engineer back in the World, but gave it up for the teams. For some reason, Stocker didn't want to be an officer either, though he had a college education.

As preparations were under way to get *Mighty Mo* headed downriver to Doung Island, unbeknown to Joynt, a province chief located on the island sent an urgent message to Saigon that was forwarded to the LST *Jennings County*. It said that the sampan with the .51 caliber machine gun would be moving that evening.

Harker notified the SEAL Team upriver in Binh Thuy of the conflicting information. He also stated in the message that they had been instructed by the powers that be in Saigon to hit the suspected target at once.

When Joynt received the message, he headed downriver with his team in two LSSCs as fast as the 427s with Jacuzzi jet pumps would go. *Mighty Mo* would never get there in time with her historically slow cruising speed. Animal had told Joynt that he was getting one of his old funny feelings. All the activity transpiring at the last minute just didn't feel right to him, and the LT always listened to Animal's funny feelings. It had saved their asses more than once.

But it was going to take place that evening, and the Seawolves couldn't wait if they were going to have a chance at catching their prey. The orders they received from Saigon had the exact canal the target would be traveling on to the main river. The message even included that there would be only two VC on the sampan, and that at most they would be armed with AK-47s.

The boat had to be hit at a certain point before it entered into a jungle-covered area where many canals, like fingers, would split up. At that point it would be difficult to tell in which direction the enemy would be headed. It would be an easy target to spot if they caught it before it reached that point.

If the Seawolves missed it, the PBRs would have a hard time catching it in the dark. Charlie, when moving something as important as this, was famous for using decoys.

For example, the U.S. Coast Guard had been patrolling the open ocean just off the tip of Doung Island with hopes of catching the Chinese junk that would be bringing the .51 caliber machine gun down. That kind of gun would be very difficult to hide. After intercepting countless junks, nothing had been found, probably because it had already been transported to the island before they set up the blockade, or because the decoys had worked.

The PBRs from the LST *Jennings County* had been concentrating their efforts on both sides of the island to make sure the smugglers couldn't get anything to the mainland. However, it was impossible to cover that much area all at once, especially at night.

Joynt knew as much, which was another reason he wanted to get downriver as fast as possible. The more people who could get on this, the more difficult it would be for Charlie to pull it off.

Harker had given both his leaders instructions to be very careful with this mission. He'd gotten a message back from the LT about Animal's funny feelings. If it hadn't still been daylight, and if they hadn't been ordered to hit this target of opportunity, he would have instructed his pilots to lay back and see what the PBRs could pick up. However, under the cover of darkness there would be a slim chance that the sampan could elude the patrol boats. The idea of that gun making it to the mainland was just too much of a risk. The mission had to be flown. They had to take their shot at stopping that gun. The U.S. Navy's best was on the job, and they would go after that gun like a one-eyed cat in a fish factory.

18

The sunset was a beautiful red as the Seawolf team prepared for the mission at hand. It was Abrams's turn to fly fire team lead on this one. Soto would have to fly cover, which meant that Abrams would get the first crack at sinking this valuable target. They were like a couple of kids, wanting to be first in line.

Nimmo was putting down the electrical contacts on the rocket pod on his side. Buddy already had his done and was sliding the M-60 barrels into his flex guns. Soto was in the pilot's seat looking over the map to double-check the location of the canal. Bagley was checking the circuit breakers and instruments. Wobbe was standing in front of his chopper, holding the rotor blade and waiting for Abrams to start the engine. Robbie was getting situated in his seat, and Romanski was finishing up with his instrument checklist. Abrams was also checking his map, like Soto.

They would fly the standard patrol at 1,000 feet just off to the south of Doung Island so they could eyeball the target area. They were hoping to see the sampan. That would make it easier to plan the gun run. If they did spot the target, they would just keep flying toward the far end of the island, to give the impression to the target boat that the choppers were just flying their normal patrol.

Once out of sight of the target, Abrams and his team would descend to a low level and double back. The Seawolves would approach the target three feet off the water back upriver until parallel to the canal, then hang a sharp right turn and pop up over the jungle, climbing out to 800 feet. Sighting the target, they would commence their gun run.

"Coming hot," Abrams yelled out his door. The jet engine was slowly starting to wind up as he pulled the trigger on the collective—which is like the starter button on a car. Wobbe held on to the main rotor blade as long as he could. As the whining noise from the jet engine got louder, the rotor blade pulled harder, until it was wrenched from his hands and started whirling faster and faster.

Wobbe took his place in the back door, pulled his helmet on, placed the barrel in his M-60, and buckled the seat belt around his body armor. Pushing his ICS button, he said, "We're clear back here, sir."

By now the helicopter was completely started and ready for liftoff. The LST sailor with the flashlights in his hands standing in front of the chopper gave the all clear to do a hover check and take off. Buddy was standing in front of his bird, holding on to his rotor blade, waiting for Abrams to depart.

As Seawolf 15 pulled up on the collective, the pitch on the rotor blades increased, taking a bigger and bigger bite out of the air, throwing it downward. The prop wash from the helicopter pushed harder on Buddy and the rotor blade he was hanging on to.

Abrams's chopper reached the lighter-than-air point and slowly came straight up off the LST's flight deck.

The wind played hell with Buddy and the LST sailor as the helicopter moved backward a little in order to get a longer run on the deck before going over the side and becoming airborne.

With the tail boom hanging over the side behind them, Abrams stopped pulling the stick back and pushed the stick forward, pulling up harder on the collective. The chopper nosed over and moved rapidly across the short deck. The LST sailor moved off to one side as the helicopter passed him.

As usual, when Seawolf 15 went over the side of the ship it dropped down several feet and then rose gracefully into the sky.

No sooner had it cleared the flight deck than Soto yelled out his door, "Coming hot!"

Seawolf 14 came alive with a familiar whine from their jet engine. The rotor blade pulled itself from Buddy's strong grip and revolved faster and faster. Buddy took his place in his seat, pulled his helmet on, locked the barrel in the M-60 in his lap, and hit his floor button. "We're ready back here, sir!"

"Roger," Soto said.

Moments later Seawolf 14 lifted into her hover check. Soto slowly scooted the aircraft backward until the boom and tail rotor hung out over the other side of the ship. Then he nosed her over and raced across the short deck, dipping down as they went over the side and once again lifted into the evening sky.

"Seawolf One-four is off at this time," Soto broadcast over the airwaves.

It wasn't long before the gunship team was flying in formation, headed for the far end of Doung Island.

● ● ●

Meanwhile, LT Joynt and his band were screaming downriver in their two LSSCs. He was in the lead boat with Animal, Outlaw, Big Daddy, and Goat, who manned the radio. Spears was driving, with Madison on the M-60. The second boat had Stocker, Mikey, Doc Stinehour, Tator, and Bullet. Barber was driving, with Phil Miner, a tech nut from Florida, on the M-60.

The sun hadn't gone totally down yet, and it was going to be a full moon that night. There wasn't a cloud in the sky, except on the horizon. Seawolf 15 was heading downriver, with Seawolf 14 staggered to the left and behind.

They were almost to the spot where they would see if they could eyeball the target. Nimmo, with his hands on his M-60, stared out toward Doung Island, along with Robbie, Bagley, and Romanski. As the two birds flew over the south bank of the island, following the river, a canal off in the distance came into view. Moving on, as an evening patrol would, they intended to get a better and better view of the canal.

Robbie was the first to spot the target. "Sir, I got him at our two o'clock!" he said over the ICS.

Romanski confirmed it: "Oh, yes, there they are, just large as life."

Abrams came up on the radio. "One-four, One-five, do you have an eye on the target? Over."

"One-five, One-four, roger!" Soto said.

"One-four, One-five, we are starting our slow descent," Abrams said.

"One-five, One-four, roger," Soto answered.

Down the two gunships went until they were out of view of the sampan. Abrams made a slow 180 and started back upriver at three feet off the water. Soto was right behind him. Nimmo, Buddy, Robbie, and Wobbe had their M-60 machine guns up at the ready, their eyes scanning the shoreline for muzzle flashes that would give the enemy position away.

Abrams had picked out a landmark on the shore of the island so he'd know where to make his right turn, and now he saw it—an old tree stump on the bank that had been uprooted by the river. He gently gave the chopper a little right rudder pedal, pulling back on the stick and to the right as he pulled up on the collective. They came to the right and climbed up over the dense jungle shoreline.

Abrams transmitted: "One-four, One-five. Three darts break left. Over."

"Roger that, One-five. Three darts with left break," Soto answered.

It didn't take long to reach 800 feet. Beneath them was the heavy jungle canopy that hid the many canals where their target could escape if they missed hitting it. The sampan came into view again just as Abrams pushed the nose over the top to start his run. As predicted, the boat had two passengers. Between them there was some kind of cargo covered by the usual banana leaves.

Robbie and Wobbe opened up with their M-60s. The two in the sampan bent over and picked up their AK-47s in an attempt to shoot back, but it was too late. The accurate machine-gun fire from the two Seawolf gunners found its mark early. The .308 caliber bullets kicked the canal water up in the air eight feet as they walked to the target and tore through the flesh of the two men on the sampan. Both bodies were wrenched from the boat as they fell lifeless into the brown water. Romanski opened up with his flex guns and started strafing the sides of the canal in case there was more enemy in the jungle. Abrams carefully lined up his sights and squeezed off the first of three rockets, then the next and the next, each time filling the compartment with sparks as they exited the tubes.

As they raced toward their target below, each rocket left a bright white trail. The first one was a high explosive round and exploded just to the left of the target, blowing a ton of water skyward. The second was a white phosphorus round and hit just to the right. The third rocket was another HE round and hit the sampan dead center, blowing it into so many toothpicks.

At 400 feet by now, Abrams broke off his run to the left. Soto's chopper opened up with its machine guns as he punched off his three rockets, to make sure there wasn't going to be anything left of the .51 caliber gun.

Pop, pop, pop, pop. The noise was followed by "We're receiving fire!" It was Nimmo over his ICS.

Soto transmitted: "One-five, One-four. We're receiving fire. Over."

"Roger that, One-four. So are we," Abrams answered.

Muzzle flashes from below were everywhere. Green and red tracers shot up and past the two choppers.

Abrams decided it was time for another run. He brought the team around and came in from the north this time. They were receiving fire from both sides of the canal that they'd just hit. "One-four, One-five, four darts break left. Over."

"Four darts left-hand break. Roger," Soto answered.

Down Abrams went again, punching off four darts.

He placed two on the near bank and two on the far bank, while his six M-60s were sending a shower of 7.62 rounds back at all the muzzle flashes. Each rocket exploding seemed to lessen the number of tracers coming back up at them. Soto was right on his tail, sending his rockets underneath Abrams's break. Each gun run was textbook perfect.

The third time, Abrams brought the chopper in from the west. This time it would be two darts sent into the last of the muzzle flashes that were still sending tracers back up. Again it was a perfect run, with the rockets right on their mark. The white phosphorus rounds left a cloud of white smoke drifting over the target area below.

That seemed to take care of the bulk of fire they'd been getting. The last run would be five darts pinpointing the area's left, where they were still getting fire from. They came from the south again.

"One-four, One-five. Five darts with a right-hand break. Over."

"Roger, One-five. Five darts with a right-hand break. I copy."

There wasn't much left of the fire coming up from the ground, so this was more of a cleanup run before they went back to the LST.

Down they went, guns blazing and rockets filling the compartment with sparks once again as they exited their tubes. Five explosions of mixed HE and WP spread out over the target area. Seawolf 15 broke off his run.

Like clockwork, Soto put the first of his last five rockets in the jungle directly underneath Abrams, to cover him breaking off his attack.

As Abrams climbed to 1,000 feet and steered for home, he thought, Outstanding. We got that damn gun.

There wasn't any more enemy gunfire coming out of the area as Soto broke off his attack. He was thinking that it was a job well done.

Then all of a sudden, *bam, bam, bam, bam, bam!* Both Robbie and Wobbe hit their ICS buttons and yelled at the same time, "We're receiving fifty fire, receiving fifty fire!" They both tossed smoke grenades out their respective doors to pinpoint where it was coming from. Then they opened up on the enemy's position right beneath them with their M-60s.

But it was too late. The Chinese Communist .51 caliber below had them dead in its sights. The few rounds that were fired walked straight through the middle of the aircraft and into the transmission in front of the jet engine. When that happens, all hope of auto rotating down safely goes right out the window. It was a perfectly placed burst of heavy machine-gun fire.

Abrams hit his transmit button, "One-four, we're receiving fifty fire, receiving fifty fire! OH, SHIT!" That was the last anyone heard from the doomed crew.

Nimmo and Buddy had also opened up on the two smoke grenades that were tossed out by Robbie and Wobbe. All that training paid off. In the face of death, which these crew were no stranger to, they had marked the location of their killer.

As Nimmo and Buddy kept firing their machine guns at the .51 caliber below, they noticed that Wobbe and Robbie were still shooting their machine guns at the target as well. All the way down, the Seawolf 14 crew could see the Seawolf 15 gunners firing. Their rotor blade had come to a complete stop because enemy fire had locked up the transmission. However, the gallant men kept fighting to the last, until the gunship disappeared under the heavy jungle canopy.

Soto switched the radio to Fox Mike so it would be transmitted all over the Delta. "This is Seawolf One-four, Mayday. This is Seawolf One-four, Mayday. Seawolf One-five has gone down. I say again, Mayday, Mayday. Seawolf One-five has gone down. Map November Charlie 4811. Zero nine degrees, thirty-seven minutes, thirty seconds. One-zero-six degrees, zero seven minutes, ten seconds. Mayday, Mayday. Seawolf One-five has gone down. . . . "

At the same time, Soto was calling out the Mayday, he was heading for the deck so they wouldn't get shot down as well. It was one of the first things he'd learned. If a big gun opened up on you and you survived, you got on the deck as fast as possible. If you were flying low level, it was harder to hit you with a big gun.

However, it did make you an easier target for small arms fire like AK-47s. Indeed, all those muzzle flashes they'd seen before, which had supposedly been shut down during the previous strikes, came right back up again.

The Seawolves weren't turning back, though. They had teammates down there somewhere, and they were going to find them. Nimmo and Buddy were burning up their barrels from all the shooting they were doing, jumping from one muzzle flash to the next as Soto maneuvered them around at treetop level, trying to find their friends.

The prop wash of a UH1-B can rock the jungle canopy, and Soto was using it as a giant hair blower to blow the jungle out of the way so they could see underneath. By now the sun had gone down and it was dusk, which made it even harder to see.

As Soto kept moving around in a hover, Bagley fired the flex guns out front and from side to side, taking on as many muzzle flashes as he could.

Nimmo and Buddy were standing out on their skids, firing their M-60s, trying desperately to stifle the enemy small arms fire and look for any sign of their friends at the same time.

Incoming rounds hit the tail boom. It sounded like someone impacting the aluminum with a hammer. Occasionally, a green tracer would fly through the compartment and continue on out the other side without hitting anything. With the limited light left, it made those tracers look like basketballs.

The large lumps in all four of their throats that they were each trying to fight back made being scared impossible. That vision of Seawolf 15 falling out of the sky with a dead still rotor blade kept replaying over and over in their minds. Rage was slowly winning out over heartbreak as the deadly skill of the men's marksmanship poured out the 7.62 bullets at 700 rounds a minute.

Then the sounds of combat were momentarily drowned out by a radio transmission: "Seawolf, Seawolf, this is Wrecking Crew. We have scrambled Wrecking Crew One and Wrecking Crew Two. Echo Tango Alpha your location approximately five mikes. Over."

Soto hit his radio button. "Wrecking Crew, Seawolf One-four. Roger. Echo Tango Alpha, five mikes. Over." That meant that they'd be there in five minutes.

Wrecking Crew was an Army gunship team out of Soc Trang. If it took them just five minutes to arrive, it meant they were already on a patrol in the area.

Another transmission came over the airwaves: "Seawolf, Seawolf. Red Tiger One. We have four slicks en route to my Lemma from Wrecking Crew. We'll have a Mike Force ready for transportation in thirty mikes to your location. Please advise on insertion point. Over."

"Roger, Red Tiger One, Seawolf One-four. Please advise when en route. Over."

That was from the Green Beret outpost located on the edge of the Bassac River, right across from Doung Island, where all this was happening. The Seawolves had saved that outpost from being overrun on several occasions.

"Seawolf One-four, Iron Hat." It was the LST *Jennings County* calling Soto. "Be advised Scorpion One has just arrived my location. He needs coordinates on crash sight and insertion point. Over."

Soto hit his transmit button. "Iron Hat, Seawolf One-four. Roger that. As soon as Wrecking Crew arrives my location we'll return. Have Seawolf One-three ready to take my place on quick turnaround. I'll stay and meet with Scorpion One. Over."

"Seawolf One-four, Iron Hat. I copy. Over."

19

Darkness had finally embraced the frustrated four men in their helicopter. There was no reason to keep flying at treetop level because they wouldn't be able to see anything anyway. Not wanting to give up the search, it was still more prudent for Soto to get the group back up to speed and move over the river before climbing to 800 feet and continuing the battle there. If they increased altitude from where they were, the big gun would pop them out of the sky as well.

Once they arrived at their higher elevation, Soto put them in an orbit around the target and gave each gunner a turn at sending machine-gun fire down at the still visible muzzle flashes coming back up at them. Bagley had depleted all his flex gun ammo and was now lobbing M-79 grenades out his door and down at the enemy below.

"Seawolf, Seawolf. Wrecking Crew One. We are on station. Where do you want it? Over."

"Wrecking Crew One, Seawolf One-four. Just put it on all those damn muzzle flashes! Over."

"That's a roger, Seawolf!"

Watching three Army Huey gunships and three

Army Cobra gunships work out on an enemy target is something to see. They carry a lot more ordnance—rockets, automatic M-79 grenade launchers, and 7.62 miniguns, which shoot 6,000 rounds per minute—than the Seawolves, because they don't have to worry about picking up passengers.

In this particular situation, Seawolf 14 couldn't stay and watch. Soto had to get back to the LST and meet with Scorpion One to plan the rescue mission. Besides, Seawolf 14 was just about out of ammo and fuel.

"Iron Hat, Seawolf One-four," Soto said. "Echo Tango Alpha five mikes for quick turnaround. Over."

"Roger, One-four. We're ready. Over."

As Soto got his chopper headed back to the LST, Joynt and his men were getting ready for insertion. One group of five men were gathered around the edge of the flight deck, by the ladder that led down to their two LSSCs. Their boats were tied up to the RPBs in the river. Another group of five was about eight paces away, over toward the middle of the LST's superstructure. Each squad was making final preparations for the job at hand.

Over by the ladder leading down to their jet boats, Animal was giving his CAR-15 the once-over, checking all his magazines of ammo, putting his silenced Smith & Wesson 22 in his shoulder holster, inventorying his grenades, and making sure the Starlight Scope was operational. Outlaw had already checked out his M-60, LAAW rocket, and grenades, along with his other miscellaneous war paraphernalia. He was now involved with putting on his camouflage war paint. Big Daddy had his M-203 ready for action, and Goat, who already had his makeup on, was just staring into the dark night, thinking about their job at hand. Lt. Joynt made sure his Stoner and all his belted ammo were wrapped around him as comfortably as possible. Spears and Madison were making sure all was ready in that group's LSSC.

Over toward the center of the LST's superstructure, Stocker was checking out the placement of his camouflage makeup, his M-203 leaning up against his leg as he squatted, gazing into a small mirror at himself. Mikey was standing next to him, readjusting all the Stoner ammunition he was carrying. His makeup was all set to go, and the LAAW rocket was slung over his shoulder. Doc Stinehour took inventory of his medical gear. He was squatting over his pack of goodies with his Stoner leaning up against an ammunition box that had contained his belted ammo. All his makeup was already on.

Tator, with his M-60 leaning against his thigh, was standing over by Stocker. His belted ammo for his M-60 was draped over him like Pancho Villa; he was making some last-minute adjustments to his camouflage paint. A LAAW rocket rested on its side by his foot. Bullet Bob, his M-60 slung over his shoulder, helped Tator with his makeup. And Vernon Barber and Phil Miner were down in their LSSC, making sure they had all their stuff together for the second squad.

The SEAL Team was ready. All they needed now was to know where to insert, the possible location of Seawolf 15 and the big gun, and where to extract.

Off in the distance they could hear the pop of Seawolf 14's rotor blades as Soto turned on final approach. The closer he got, the louder the sound. All the red lights were lit up on the flight deck so Soto could see, and a man with flashlights in his hands stood in the middle of the flight deck to give the pilot directions to the exact spot on the deck to set the bird down.

As the chopper came in ever so slowly over the river, the wind picked up and almost blew the SEAL Team's hats off. They had their hands on their hats to keep it from happening.

Soto's helicopter appeared out of the night sky and hovered in over the deck. Moving slowly to the directions of the deckhand and his flashlights, Soto skillfully set his bird down exactly where he was directed.

As the bird sat there, the flight deck crew ran out to help Nimmo and Buddy reload their bird with fuel, rockets, and ammunition. Lieutenant Minnahan ran out of the officers' quarters and over to the gunship. Soto climbed out of his pilot's seat to turn Seawolf 14 over to Seawolf 13.

Minnahan was taking over so Soto could meet with LT Joynt. That way, returning to the battle wouldn't be held up while questions were being asked and answered as to the whereabouts of Seawolf 15, the suspected location of the big gun, and directions to the insertion and extraction points.

The relief pilot in place, rockets, ammunition, and fuel all reloaded, it was time for liftoff. Soto and Joynt were going over the maps as Minnahan pulled up into a hover and the wind picked up around the chopper. The popping sound got much louder as the gunship accelerated across the short deck and over the side. Once again the Seawolf chopper disappeared into the night sky, heading back to the site where their friends had left them so unexpectedly.

Soto, Joynt, and the rest of the team stared at the

map, memorizing its complex diagram of where they were headed. All ten SEALs had to know exactly who, what, where, when, and how.

The discussion was to the point and short.

It was time for the team to depart. They needed to find the possibly doomed crew ASAP. The ten hunters and shooters went over the side and down the ladder. They made their way over the parked PBRs and out to where their jet boats were tied up.

Armed to the teeth, each squad of five got situated in their respective LSSCs. Miner untied his boat as Madison untied his. Then they each took their places, their M-60s at the ready.

Floating free of the large ship, both Spears and Barber slammed their throttles to the wall. Coming up to speed almost instantly, the two LSSCs were swallowed up by the darkness of the Bassac River.

Meanwhile, the Mike Force at the Green Beret base were putting camouflage paint on their faces and getting their shit together as they waited for their Army choppers to arrive. It was going to be a quick flight across the river to the island and their insertion point. The SEAL Team would be in the jungle before the Army's Special Forces were airborne.

Since the SEAL Team would be operating with Green Beret and Army gunships, radioman Goat would have to use their frequency instead of the secured one in the PRC-25. Not that it was a problem. At that point, the enemy knew what was going on. This would be a "balls to the wall" hunt-and-shoot mission all the way.

With the moon out, it was a clear night, so the shoreline could be seen fairly well. Even so, Spears kept one eye on the radarscope and the other on steering the fast-moving yet silent boat as they closed in on Doung Island. Barber was right behind him, maneuvering his LSSC as if both boats were attached.

Off in the distance they could see the firefight raging on between the Army gunships in the air and the VC on the ground, green tracers going up and red tracers going down. There was no doubt when a rocket was launched toward the enemy positions since they left a bright white tail as they screamed for their targets below. When they exploded on impact, there was a large flash in the night sky.

The miniguns mounted on the noses of the Cobras were something to see at night. Six thousand rounds a minute made it look like a laser beam being shot at the ground. And the sound they made was frightening. They didn't go rat-a-tat; instead, it was an eerie roar.

The other Army UH1-C gunships had automatic M-79 grenade launchers mounted in their noses. When they opened up, it was an incredible fireworks display of death—hundreds of little explosions lighting up the jungle.

Each gun run the Army made was answered with green tracers coming back up from a different position. One thing missing from the mix, however, was the Chinese Communist .51 caliber machine gun.

As the SEALs flew across the water toward their destination, they couldn't help but wonder what had happened to the big gun. Why wasn't it firing at the Army's onslaught?

20

Spears had found the canal they were looking for on the radarscope and was heading for shore. Joynt and his men were restless. The crazy Seawolves had saved all ten SEALs at one time or another, and the ten were ready for a little payback. No, a whole shitload of payback.

The canal was about twenty feet wide as the two jet boats slowed and entered the mouth of the waterway. The jungle was very thick on both sides, with a short mud bank. Madison on his M-60 was scanning the left side, and Miner, in the trailing boat, was scanning the right side with his M-60. The SEALs were tense as they waited for the signal to disembark.

Spears led them in about a hundred yards until he came to a fork in the canal. Joynt signaled Spears to drop his team off in the middle of the split. Instinctively, Barber brought his boat up to the right of Spears', and both LSSCs silently slid up onto the mud bank next to each other. Madison kept his focus to the jungle on the left and Miner did the same to the right.

They could hear the firefight continuing off in the distance. It was much louder now that they had closed in on the target.

Good old reliable Brent "Animal" Ellison was the

first out on the mud bank. His large frame entered the jungle in a fluid motion that radiated confidence. His face and bald head were painted black and green, giving it the appearance of a skull. Wearing a tiger-striped top that had both sleeves ripped off, exposing painted black and green muscle-popping arms, he moved quickly, feeling for booby traps. Across his massive chest, his web gear supported several fifty-round magazines of .223 caliber bullets, a silenced Smith & Wesson, numerous grenades, a medical pouch, and a K-bar knife. Across his back were more magazines and his Starlight Scope. In one hand he held his CAR-15, safety off and ready to rock and roll, and he watched 180 degrees in front as he moved forward in a fast walk.

Joynt, heavily armed, as usual on such a mission, was next on the mud bank. His eaglelike eyes covered their advance to the left. Then came Outlaw, holding his M-60 machine gun at the ready and covering their right as they advanced into the jungle at a fast walk. Then Goat covering to the left with an M-203. Big Daddy Diamond was the last out of Spears's boat, covering the right with his M-203.

Spears backed his boat off the bank and spun it like a top so he faced out of the area. He stopped there, waiting for Barber.

Stocker hit the shore next. Wearing a tiger-striped floppy hat, painted face, tiger-striped shirt, and blue jeans with tennis shoes, he proceeded in a fast walk at line-of-sight distance behind Big Daddy. He carried an M-203, covering to the left. His web gear was the same as Big Daddy's. He also had a LAAW rocket over his shoulder, with a satchel charge as well.

Mikey came next, covering the right and carrying a

Stoner. Doc Stinehour, with the medical pack on his back, covered the left. Tator Hanson's machine gun was pointed to the right as he entered the jungle. And then came Bullet Crenshaw, the last out of Barber's boat, covering 180 degrees to the rear of the platoon with an M-60 machine gun.

Barber backed his LSSC off the bank and spun it around just in time to see Spears go to full throttle. Both jet boats exited back onto the Bassac River in a matter of seconds. Meanwhile, *Mighty Mo* had been heading down from Binh Thuy. It wouldn't be much longer before she would be in place to meet up with Spears and Barber. Once they hooked up, it would be time to head for the extraction point on the other side of Doung Island, where a larger canal wound back and forth up to a spot two klicks farther down from where the battle was taking place.

All ten of the SEALs were moving rapidly through the thick jungle toward the covered canopy area where the target canal split up into many exit points leading back to the side of the island where they had inserted. They advanced in a zigzag search pattern so as not to miss a thing.

Unfortunately, the exact location of the downed Seawolf was not known, which didn't make the mission any easier.

Animal, with his sixth sense, was moving like a jungle cat hot on the trail of his prey. He could tell he was getting close because the sounds of battle were getting louder. Then he saw the back of a black-pajama-clad Viet Cong who was intent on looking up, trying to get a shot at one of the circling helicopters with his AK-47.

Animal was on him like a bad habit. Letting his

CAR-15 hang by his side on his sling, he grabbed the VC's head from behind with his two hands and snapped his neck like a twig, dropping him to the ground and moving on all in one smooth motion, as if merely slapping some jungle undergrowth out of the way.

Joynt stepped over the body and kept on moving, as did Outlaw, Goat, and Big Daddy.

Once again Animal had his CAR-15 up at the ready. Moving at his fast walking pace, he was confronted with another VC. This one came from his left and turned straight for him, as if he were headed for the VC Animal had just killed. With his AK-47 in hand and pointed at Animal, the VC stopped abruptly, seeing the huge muscle-bound charging figure with the green and black skull face. He froze in sheer terror as Animal closed the distance on him. At point-blank range, Animal squeezed off a three-round burst from his CAR-15 in the man's face, and the VC's head popped like a large water balloon, spraying Animal with brain matter. Animal was moving so fast that he had to give the falling body a shoulder block to get it out of the way as he continued on. Joynt and the rest moved past body number two.

Then Animal came to a screeching halt. Using hand signals, he notified the rest of the team that there was a canal in front of him. Looking both ways to make sure all was clear, he proceeded across. He didn't like doing it, but he knew the Seawolves were waiting anxiously for some news of their fallen comrades. Time was not a luxury they could afford.

The water was shoulder deep as Animal made his way across. Once on the other side, he covered Joynt as he crossed, followed by the rest of the platoon. It was the first of the many tributaries that were hidden by the jungle canopy.

They could hear shooting all around now, as well as the explosions of rockets and M-79s that the Army choppers above were sending down into the jungle. It wouldn't be much longer before Goat would have to call the air cover off so the team wouldn't be hit by their own guys. So far, though, it made for a good distraction, which helped their rapid advance into the target area.

Moving on through the jungle in search of the next canal, more VC started popping up. Tator spotted two on his right and dismembered them with his M-60. Then one came up on them from behind, and Bullet blew him back into the jungle. All the training was paying off. The SEALs had seen the VC first, and he who sees first lives.

Moving on farther in their zigzag pattern helped keep them unpredictable. If Charlie expected anything, they'd play hell trying to figure out where the next green face might pop up. Sure enough, Mikey got the next one on his right. A short burst from his Stoner dropped two sets of black pajamas to the ground. It appeared that the enemy was starting to expect something now, because the last two weren't looking up in the sky. They were looking for something or someone in the jungle.

Goat got the next two who made the mistake of popping up in front on his left. It took a little longer burst from his M-203 to take them out because they were ready and waiting for a ground target.

Then Animal signaled that he'd found another canal. Still no sign of the Seawolf helicopter. As he set up to start across, he noticed a movement down in the darkness of the waterway to his left. Unable to see that far, he slung the Starlight Scope around and pulled it up to his eye. Peering through the lens, he made out a sampan moving their way. Quickly, with hand signals, he passed the news to the rest of the platoon. Joynt made the call with his hand signals to set up a skirmish line in preparation to take out the approaching target.

By the time they got set up, the slow-moving sampan was on top of them. It was a large one with two men on board. It was powered by a Chinese outboard motor and was moving like a trolling motor would move a bass boat back in the World. There was definitely cargo of some kind covered up in the middle of the boat.

Joynt gave instructions that they had to do this quietly because of all the attention they were starting to get. They needed time to search the craft before they moved on. Animal, Big Daddy, and Stocker would use their silenced Smith & Wessons to take out the VC. Then they'd stop the sampan and board her. The canal was narrow, so they wouldn't be shooting too far. Coupled with the lack of light, they'd take one target at a time just to make sure.

On Joynt's mark, all three SEALs opened up first on the VC operating the motor. He dropped like a stone. Just as the other VC pulled up his AK-47, the three silencers, each double tapping, riddled his head, dropping him into the bottom of the boat.

Tator and Doc were already moving out into the canal to stop the forward motion of their target. As they climbed aboard, the others were setting up a perimeter to cover the searching of the cargo.

It didn't take long to figure out that it was a decoy.

As the team digested this, they all got a terrible thought. The big gun could have been transported out of the area while all this was going on. That's why it never opened up on the other choppers in the air.

As the team moved on, leaving the sampan adrift with its two dead VC, they were all thinking the same thing. Their Seawolf brothers had been set up.

The Seawolves had a bounty on their heads, just as the SEALs did. Somewhere around $10,000 a head.

It was the same age-old trick. Hit and run. Undoubtedly the enemy had used the false information that was passed to Saigon to suck their target in, hit them, and wrap up the big gun to use another day.

What they didn't expect was the SEALs having such a fast response time. The enemy probably still hadn't expected that the possible target they had on the ground was "the men with the green faces." They probably thought it was an ARVN group that was stationed close by, who usually didn't get much respect from the VC.

By the time Bullet, covering the rear, started to disappear into the jungle's edge at the canal they just left, he saw a shitload of VC show up on the far bank. Since they weren't shooting at him, he figured they hadn't seen him. That's good, he thought. I can always kill them later. So he became part of the jungle and disappeared, still watching their rear. However, he did notify the rest of the platoon about what was going on behind them.

With the latest news passed up to Animal, he picked up the pace. He was thinking it was a good call by the LT to take out the sampan quietly. It could have been a disaster if they'd hit the sampan with a lot of noise.

Still looking for the downed Seawolf helicopter and

its crew, Animal came upon another one of the many tributaries. Checking as carefully as he had time to spare, he proceeded across. Again it was shoulder-deep water. Doing the usual cross and cover maneuver, the team had just about put the tributary behind them when a signal from Tator came up to Animal that they had spotted another sampan.

Backtracking, the team set up another skirmish line. As before, they did it quietly. Luckily, this target was moving slower than the last one. That gave them more time to get in place.

After the two tangos—or targets—in the boat had been neutralized, Outlaw and Stocker climbed aboard to search the cargo. Jackpot! It was the big gun!

Stocker signaled Big Daddy to toss him his satchel charge. With his and Big Daddy's charges and timers set, he and Outlaw exited into the jungle. But not before they locked the outboard motor in place so it would continue on down the canal. Two satchel charges would turn that .51 caliber gun into twisted metal garbage.

Again as Bullet disappeared into the jungle, he saw the same group of VC on the other bank. They didn't spot him this time either.

This particular situation required a different response. Passing the info on to the rest of the team, Joynt decided it was time to hit the VC. For one thing, the Army was starting to come too close to their location with their heavy air support. Also, they wanted to make sure that gun was taken care of.

Setting up a fast skirmish line, Joynt signaled, with his first shot, to open up. By then the VC were halfway across the canal. It was a perfect ambush.

Joynt's Stoner sang out, and almost immediately

three M-60s, three M-203s, a CAR-15, and two more Stoners started singing their song all on full automatic. Eight VC in the canal, six on the far side just entering the canal, and six more on the far bank dropped without firing a shot.

With that out of the way, the ten SEALs waited for what would come next. They didn't have to wait long. The wandering sampan had made its way down the straight canal until it was turned into toothpicks when the satchel charges went off. The explosion was enormous, as was the shock wave that was sent through the waiting SEALs lying on the ground.

Pieces of steel and wood came showering down from the sky, spreading out on the canal, the jungle, and the SEALs. It took a minute before the team could recover and continue their search.

Joynt instructed Goat to break radio silence, to contact Wrecking Crew and tell them to discontinue their strikes. Some of their M-79s and rockets had come too close to the team's location. They'd felt the blasts all around them, which meant it was time to stop all that help, and fast.

They knew that now, without the air cover, the enemy's attention would be turned to them. Animal picked up the pace once again. The zigzag search pattern still hadn't turned up anything.

But then the whole team started picking up tangos everywhere. Still moving through the jungle at a good pace, all ten men were dropping Viet Cong in their assigned areas as regular as clockwork. Joynt was thinking, This is getting way too thick.

Animal signaled back that he'd found another canal and in the middle of it was what used to be a Seawolf helicopter. All guns blazing, the SEAL Team moved on to the crash site and set up a defensive position around it.

Joynt got Goat over next to him and jumped on the radio: "Wrecking Crew, Wrecking Crew. Scorpion One. We have attained objective. Follow the green and red tracer fire to spot our location. We are under heavy fire. I repeat, we are under heavy fire. Over!"

"Scorpion One, Wrecking Crew Four. We are en route to your location. Over."

En route to my location! Joynt was thinking. What's with that shit? They were just up there! But that was Wrecking Crew One and Two. They must have run out of ammo about the time they were called off.

Joynt got back on the radio. "Wrecking Crew Four, Scorpion One. What's your Echo Tango Alpha? Over."

"Scorpion One, Wrecking Crew Four. Ten mikes. Over."

"Well, fuck me," Joynt said. Back on the radio, he said, "Roger, Wrecking Crew."

He was thinking, Shit, we've got to have enough firepower to get us to the extraction point. This was not looking good.

While the other nine SEALs were returning fire into the jungle on all sides, Joynt slid down into the canal and pulled a quick inventory on the Seawolves. All four of the crew were still in the wreckage. As far as he could tell, they never felt a thing. They all had to have died on impact. One thing was missing, though. All their weapons were gone. The chopper had been completely stripped.

Shaking off the hate he was feeling from what had happened to his brothers, he slid back up into position and started returning fire with the rest.

The six SEALs who had LAAW rockets picked out the heaviest concentration of fire they were getting and started using their rockets to surprise Charlie. Each time a rocket was used, the enemy fire died off considerably, then would slowly pick back up again.

Goat's radio came alive with a new contact: "Scorpion One, Scorpion One. Red Tiger One, Red Tiger One. Over."

Not getting his hopes up, Joynt got back on the radio. "Red Tiger One, Scorpion One. Over."

"Scorpion, Red Tiger. I'm marking my location at your six o'clock position with tracer fire. Please confirm. Over."

Joynt turned around and looked toward the sky at his six o'clock position. With a completely shocked expression, followed by one of joy, he saw a stream of red tracers climb skyward less than fifty yards from his location. Jumping back on the radio, he said, "Roger that, Red Tiger, I confirm red tracers. Over."

"Scorpion, Red Tiger. Hold your fire. We're coming in. Over."

Joynt signaled the team to hold up fire at their six o'clock position due to friendlies coming in. "Roger, Red Tiger. You're clear. Scorpion out."

It was an incredible sight for the ten SEALs to see a Mike Force of Green Berets come charging to aid in their defense, though by now it was more of an offense, what with incoming enemy fire slowly dwindling to nothing.

The LT in charge of the Mike Force made his way over to Joynt and introduced himself: "How's it goin', SEAL? They call me Jimmy."

"Stuart Joynt here, and I'm damn glad to see ya! How in hell did you guys find us?"

"Shit, that was easy. We just followed the dead bodies."

Now that all was secure, Seawolf 14 helped guide Scorpion One to the extraction point. Their only injuries were cuts and bruises from the two satchel charges going off in the sampan, destroying the big gun.

The Green Berets provided security for their fallen comrades till morning, when the Army brought in a Chinook helicopter that lifted the four men and their downed aircraft out of the jungle.

Before those four brave men went to be with Jesus, they had saved a lot of others to go on to do more good things. Their time was up here on earth, but I have to believe we'll see them again when the final trumpet sounds.

21

It was a beautiful afternoon, with the sun shining down on the South Vietnam city of Vung Tau. The dry season was in full swing. All the paved streets were covered with dry red dust, which blew around slowly with the slight breeze coming off the ocean. Here in this tropical paradise, the heat would have been unbearable if not for that breeze. It was a saving grace for the troops stationed there.

Commander Spencer had called his regularly scheduled monthly get-together in Vung Tau at the Seawolf BOQ located just off base. All the officers in charge of each detachment had flown in. Once the meeting had been called to order, there was a moment of silent prayer for their lost brothers in this crazy war called a police action.

The results of this meeting were positive since the casualty rate of the Seawolves was comparatively small. It had gone from around eighty percent down to somewhere around ten percent. That wasn't bad, considering that the enemy casualties were around 2,500, plus two thousand vessels sunk and somewhere around 2,800 VC structures destroyed. That didn't count the several thousand enemy arms captured by the combined efforts of the River Rats, SEALs, and

Seawolves. The intelligence that had been gathered was formidable. This newly found "brown water navy unit" was taking it to the Vietnamese Communists in a big way.

There were many reasons for the Seawolves' success. One was the new attack procedure that had been outlined by Spencer, which was taken from his days as a fighter pilot in the Korean War. Another reason was that all seven detachments were run like families. The enlisted gunners were the kids, the pilots were their big brothers, and the commander of the detachment was the dad. There was never any saluting, but the respect for the higher rank was there. Also, the relationship between each detachment was that of a very strong brotherhood.

It was as simple as the dress code, or rather, the lack of it. Shaves and haircuts were also optional. Each person had his own individual look. That was permitted as long as the men performed as they were supposed to. In fact, the teams performed above and beyond the call of duty.

It gave the men a feeling of being special, which of course they were. When a team went into Vung Tau for maintenance or whatever, they stood out from the rest of the military personnel on the base. They also got "head of the line" privileges in the base chow hall. It's amazing how well people will perform for just a little recognition. Certainly, you couldn't argue with the results.

Once new goals had been set for all seven detachments, it was time to adjourn the meeting and take it across the street, to the Dragon Lady's bar. It was time for the reality of war to be forgotten for the night and to enjoy a bit of fantasyland.

The order of the day was to get silly and laugh as much as possible. If it wasn't for that, they would have had to be put away in some institution for the totally depressed. Tomorrow would be a new day of killing, and now was not the time for thinking about it.

However, once everyone had their first drink in hand, the question of medals came up. The fact was, no one was doing the required paperwork for the awards, so they couldn't be issued. In other words, acts of incredible bravery were not being recognized. On top of that, the U.S. Navy's criteria for issuing decorations for bravery were considerably stiffer than in the rest of the armed forces.

The men out in the trenches were just doing their job naturally, without expecting any special reward. Spencer knew that was a great attitude to have. He also knew that, years later, when they would be looking back on these days, they would need to have their medals of valor. It would be very important to them. And so he made it clear that the paperwork situation had to be rectified. Still, as a result of the inadequacies in the past, a lot of men were overlooked because their selfless acts of bravery were not a matter of record.

Anyway, as the dual party/meeting continued, some puppies came out of the back room and were wandering around on the barroom floor. Jack Bolton moved the group's discussion toward the little critters that had unexpectedly invaded the after-hour conference room. He counted seven little fur balls and said, "Hey, guys, we've been needing a mascot for some time now. How about these puppies?"

Fury chimed in with, "That's a great idea. There's just enough to go around too."

Bolton asked the Dragon Lady if it would be all right to take the seven little cuties off her hands.

Her answer was the wrong thing to say to our soft-hearted group. She told them that she was fattening them up on rice so at a later date she could use them for food.

That wasn't going to fly with the men.

Much later that night, when the Dragon Lady had closed up shop, everyone moved the meeting back across the street to the BOQ. Spencer and the XO had packed it in when Bolton brought up the idea of mascots once again. The others were all on the same page. There was no way they were going to let the Dragon Lady slaughter those cute little mutts. After several more rounds of one hundred proof, it was time for a covert operation.

The conspirators consisted of seven lieutenant commanders and seven lieutenant junior grades—a total of fourteen of the United States Navy's finest, who were drunker than a hooter owl. Some were wearing tiger-striped fatigues, some wore olive drab fatigues, some had cutoffs, and some wore the Navy issue flight suits. Some had floppy hats on, like the men in the SEAL teams wore, and some were wearing the type of hat worn in the Marine Corps. Some didn't have a hat at all.

The motley-looking crew planned to sneak back across the street after midnight. All the windows and doors were locked, so they'd have to find another way in. Tunneling under the building was out. That left the roof as the only other option. They'd have to find a way in from the roof. But first they'd have to find a way to get up to the roof.

All fourteen guys quietly snuck out the front door

of the BOQ. The last thing they needed was to wake up the skipper. Next, they had to deal with the enlisted Seawolf pulling guard duty at the front gate. Bolton approached the young sentry and said, "At ease, son. What you are about to be witness to, you're not a witness to. Do you understand?"

"Yes, sir!" the nineteen-year-old from New York answered.

"Good," Bolton said. "Okay, boys, follow me."

With that, he proceeded across the street, with Fury hot on his heels. Luscher was right behind Fury, and Reardon was behind Luscher, and Keyes was behind Reardon. And the rest were behind them.

The young sentry was doing all he could to keep from laughing out loud as he watched the fourteen heroes stagger into the darkness across the street. He was thinking, What the fuck are these nuts up to anyway?

Bolton was staggering around in the dark, trying to find a way to the roof. It seemed to him there had to be a way. As he moved cautiously around to the back of the building, he found a steel ladder that was bolted to the side of the stucco wall. It went up to a balcony on the second floor, like a fire escape. There was just enough moonlight to make out a railing around the balcony that could be used as a step to get to the roof—that is, if they couldn't get in through the door that was on the second-floor balcony.

The thirteen cat—or rather, dog—burglars behind him were anything but. They were staggering around in the dark, giggling like a bunch of Cub Scouts going on their first panty raid. It was a wonder that they weren't waking up the whole neighborhood.

Bolton made it up the ladder and tried the door. No

luck; it was locked. As Fury made it up the ladder to
Bolton's position, Bolton was stepping onto the railing, which also included stepping on Fury's fingers,
and pulling himself up to the roof. Once there, he
helped Fury up, and Fury pulled Luscher up, and so
on until all fourteen stood proudly on the top of the
Dragon Lady's villa.

"Now that we're all up here, how in hell do we get
in?" Keyes asked.

Bolton, laughing under his breath, said, "How the
fuck should I know?"

All fourteen spread out, scouring the rooftop for a
way in. Reardon was the first to find a possibility. He
whispered to the rest, or what he thought was a whisper: "Hey, guys, over here. There's some kind of attic
access hatch here or something." He was so loud, the
young sentry across the street probably heard him.

They all gathered around the small spot and looked
at the metal hatch Reardon had found.

It should be noted that this was a two-story building built by Vietnamese, for Vietnamese. The Vietnamese are generally not very big, nor do they weigh
much. And this rooftop now held fourteen full-grown
men from America who averaged about 180 pounds
each, for an approximate total of 2,520 pounds,
standing in a space that was about sixteen square feet.

"What's that sound?" Keyes asked the others.

Luscher said, "It sounds like something is breaking."

No sooner were the words out of his mouth than all
fourteen found themselves crashing through the roof
and into the main sleeping quarters of the Dragon
Lady's hookers.

Screams shrieked out in the night. It sounded like

the world had just come to an end. The fourteen burglars probably wished it had.

Naked women were running everywhere, and the fourteen were tripping over them. Seven puppies were yelping for their lives and peeing all over the place as they ran. Naked women were slipping in pee and falling down. The fourteen were getting peed on as they grabbed up the seven puppies. The Dragon Lady was yelling at the Americans as they found the stairs and slipped and fell down them to the first floor. She couldn't catch them because of all the naked ladies still panicking and slipping in the pee.

Once on the ground floor, the fourteen burglars hit the front door with such force, the lock never had a chance.

Out they went, into and across the street, past the young sentry and into the BOQ with puppies squealing all the way. The poor sentry had no idea what had just taken place as he stood there with a shocked expression on his face.

By the time the Dragon Lady made it to the street, all was quiet, not a creature stirring. She never did figure out what had happened, but she did have her suspicions.

22

The Green Beret outpost on the Gulf of Siam up next to the Cambodian border, being soaked by the rains of the monsoon season, is located at the top of a hill, with nothing but mud surrounding it. There's a flat area just big enough for two helicopters to land at the foot of the hill, on the side that faces the gulf. The other three sides face jungle about 200 yards away. Between the outpost walls and the jungle there's a giant mud pond.

It's about noontime and the rain is really coming down. The ceiling, or cloud cover, is very low, no more than about 300 or 400 feet.

Standing out in the rain with the usual Green Beret sentries are two men on the top of the perimeter wall. They're both looking out into the gulf as if waiting for something.

One is Green Beret Captain Scot Carpenter. He's six feet two inches of slender tough guy, wears the usual olive drab fatigues bloused neatly into his jump boots and an olive drab Army floppy hat that hangs down around his head, soaked with the rain that is still falling. He has the usual Army Special Forces patches, silver jump wings, and captain's bars on his uniform.

Standing next to him is a Marine Corps recon lieutenant by the name of David Owen. He's five feet ten inches of the usual Marine muscle-bound build. He wears tiger-striped fatigues bloused into jungle boots and a Marine Corps tiger-striped hat, also hanging limp due to the heavy rain.

Neither man is saying a word. They're just standing there, waiting for something. As they look out into the overcast, empty sky they detect a faint sound. It's a fast popping sound. As it gets louder, the two men see a faint image appear in all the gray stuff out in the gulf. It takes shape slowly as it gets closer. The view they have is a black, white, and gray image. It's the outline of two helicopter gunships. It's an eerie image, the way they start to appear coming straight at you out of the low clouds.

Sure enough, it's just what they're waiting for: two Seawolf helicopter gunships with a SEAL Team squad on board, arriving right on schedule.

As the choppers get closer, they slow considerably. Coming in over the water, they almost slow to a hover, tossing water mist out and away, then up and back down through the rotor blades. Each gunship comes in side by side to the flat spot at the bottom of the hill. The tail booms dip, as if to curtsy, just before setting down in the mud. The operators that had been ordered have finally arrived. It's time to get to work.

The jet engines slowly whine down as they're turned off. The rotor blades slow as the passengers start to emerge from the choppers. Unloading from the two Seawolf helicopters are eight SEALs and eight Seawolves.

The SEALs are Lieutenant Richard Benedict; Chief Petty Officer Animal Ellison; First Class Petty Officer

Tom Moloney; Second Class Petty Officers Fritz Heitjan, Kyle Anderson, and Kane Kennedy, the radioman;
First Class Petty Officer Medic Richard Oliver; and
Second Class Petty Officer Eric Red, newly added to
the platoon. The new man stands six-foot-four and
weighs in at a muscular 235 pounds. He was born and
raised in San Antonio, Texas, and loves the good old
outdoor life.

The Seawolves in the lead bird are pilot Lieutenant
Commander Bill Harker, copilot Lieutenant Junior
Grade Chuck Bagley, and two gunners—Second Class
Petty Officers Steve "Mack" McAllister and Mike
"O.B." O'Boyle. The trail bird's pilot is Lieutenant
Jim Beam. His copilot is Lieutenant Junior Grade
Noel "Hollywood" Campbell. Their gunners are Sec-
ond Class Petty Officers Lyle Nimmo and Fred
"Buddy" Record.

The rotor blades, completely stopped now, are tied
down, and the group slowly makes its way up the
muddy incline to the two waiting officers. After introductions are made, they go inside to review the mission at hand.

Lieutenant Owens's recon platoon had been doing
jumps into Cambodia to try and collect intel. The latest prisoner snatch turned up a "Chuy Hoi"—a defec-
tor. They call the Chuy Hoi "Johnny," for "Johnny on
the spot," because it seems he has valuable information. Something big is coming up, and he's going to
lead the U.S. forces to the person who knows about it.

Which is where the SEAL and Seawolf teams come
in. Since they have a good operating record, especially
in bad weather, Johnny is going to show them where
they can pick up the guy that has all the answers.

There's one problem, though. The guy is in Cambodia, and the operation to retrieve him will take place that night. Johnny shows our guys on the map where this tango will be. He'll be traveling alone in a sampan down a certain narrow canal at about 0200 hours on his way to a big meeting. The team will have to grab him before he gets there and jump back across the border before getting caught.

Benedict says, "That's not a problem. Johnny's going with us just in case he's full o' shit. We wouldn't want any surprises, and if we got one, we'd want to make sure Johnny gets his also. After all, we are an equal opportunity employer."

The plan is set. Harker and his team will depart at 2300 hours, with Benedict and his team on board. They'll fly at low level over the border about three klicks in. The drop will be north of the target canal about one klick. Harker's team will fly back across the border and south about two klicks, landing and waiting in a rice paddy until it's time to extract Benedict's guys. The SEAL Team squad will hump it for one klick south and set up on the canal. After grabbing the tango, they'll hoof it south for another klick, where Harker and his guys will pick them all up again. Sounds simple enough.

The rest of the day is spent sleeping for the night's operation. Nimmo, Mack, Buddy, and O.B. go back down the muddy hill and snooze in their two choppers, listening to the rainfall. Harker, Bagley, Beam, Hollywood, and Benedict crash in the officers' quarters. The rest of the SEAL Team rests in the enlisted quarters.

There's nothing like sleeping under a metal roof when it's raining outside. It kind of makes you think of home. It's very relaxing. One problem, though—it never lasts long enough.

So much for sleep. It's time to get up and prepare for the mission at hand.

While Nimmo, Buddy, Mack, and O.B. do a pre-flight on their birds, the SEAL Team gets suited up and puts on their war paint.

Benedict and Animal have checked their CAR-15s and are now helping each other with the makeup. Moloney and Anderson are arranging and rearranging their Stoner belted ammunition around their waists and crisscrossing their chests. Eric Red and Fritz have already loaded themselves down with enough ammunition for their M-60s and are now working on the war paint. Oliver, done with his war paint, loads himself down with all his M-60 ammo, then goes through his medical gear. Kennedy has finished his makeup and checking his M-203 and is now double-checking his PRC-25 radio. "Johnny on the spot" isn't getting a weapon. He's just along for the ride. It's up to him if he makes a round trip of it.

Eric looks over at Animal, standing there with his usual stuff on: high-water tiger-striped pants and high-top tennis shoes, tiger-striped top with the sleeves torn off and his arms painted black and green, web gear loaded down with extra magazines and grenades of all types, bald head painted like a black and green skull. And in his hand he has his CAR-15, which is dwarfed by his arms.

Eric says, "Aren't you worried about those bare arms? That tall elephant grass over there in Cambodia is going to give you one hell of a lot of paper cuts to beat the band."

Animal just looks back at him as if to say, "And your point?"

Eric shakes his head and continues to double-check his stuff.

"Saddle up, guys, it's time to go," Benedict says.

As the SEAL Team makes its way out into the rain, across the muddy yard, and toward the perimeter of the outpost, Harker and the other pilots are already in their birds, checking and double-checking their maps to make sure they know exactly where they're going. After all, this whole mission is going to be flown at low level and in the dark, and with questionable weather conditions. Back in those days, there weren't helmets with night vision glasses in them. The men had to just rely on their own eyes, their instruments, and fly by the seat of their pants.

Buddy unties the main rotor blade and walks it around front. Nimmo is putting in the flex gun barrels. Mack walks their bird's rotor blade around in front of Beam as O.B. sticks in their flex gun barrels. Harker yells out his window, "Clear, coming hot!"

Beam yells out his window, "Clear, coming hot!"

Both jet engines start to whine up. The rotor blades are pulled from both gunners' hands and around they go, faster and faster. Nimmo and Buddy get set in their bird with Harker and Bagley. Mack and O.B. are set in their seats behind Beam and Hollywood.

By the time Benedict and his crew get down the muddy bank in the pouring rain, the two Seawolf choppers are already turning up full speed.

Animal, Moloney, Fritz, and Benedict climb in Harker's bird. Animal pulls Johnny along.

Kennedy, Oliver, Anderson, and Eric climb in Beam's bird.

Nimmo hits his ICS button, says, "We're already back here, boss."

"Roger that. Coming up for hover check," Harker answers.

You can hear the helicopter strain under the extra weight on board as the rotor blades take a bigger and bigger chunk of the sky, trying to lift the chopper up.

O.B. hits his ICS button. "We're all ready to go back here, boss."

"I gotcha. Coming up for hover check," he answers.

Both birds are in a five-foot hover now and slowly turning to the right, staying in their hover positions. That lines up Harker in the lead and Beam straight behind him at his six o'clock. Harker has minimum running lights going so Beam can see him. Remember, it's nighttime with a heavy cloud cover and lots of rain still coming down. Beam's going to have to stay close so as not to lose him in the night. Harker and Beam have their red instrument lights turned down as much as possible, so it won't hinder their night vision, while still being bright enough to be able to read them. If they're not careful, this could be the shortest trip in history.

Both gunners on both birds just have half a cheek of their butts on their seats. The rest of their bodies are outside, giving the SEALs more room inside.

Harker slowly tips his bird forward. Beam follows suit, in order to stick to him like glue. The way those two operate, you'd think they were the Blue Angels.

Ever so slowly, the two helicopters move off the flat part of the mud and over to the main part of the land. Once there, Harker pushes his stick forward just a little more and pulls up on the collective a little more, increasing the pitch on the rotor blade even further.

That makes the helicopter gain speed. Beam is right on his tail.

Now heading toward the far jungle, they're finally picking up some good speed. As they do, they gain a little altitude. They come up to about 25 feet. It's a scary altitude, considering the weather. Luckily, there's a full moon out. You can't see it because of the cloud cover, but it does let a little light through—just enough for the eagle-eyed pilots to see where they're going. The navigation is critical. All their Navy pilot training is being put to the test. Taking up a heading with the wind speed and direction tells them how long to fly in that direction before they turn onto their second heading.

The Navy pilots can always find an aircraft carrier blindfolded, at night and in a storm, and land safely. That's why they're the Navy!

The gunners on each side keep their eyes peeled as well, looking for tall trees and anything else in their way that their pilots might fail to see.

Approaching the jungle moving north, each chopper comes up and over the trees without incident. Now it's a matter of staying as low as possible and not running into anything. That means dodging the taller trees and skipping across the tops of the shorter ones. It's a case of follow the leader as each gunship dips here and there and jogs this way and that as the gunners and copilots use the intercom system to help direct the pilot.

They go farther and farther north, the four gunners standing outside on the rocket pod, M-60s on their shoulders, taking a hard rainfall in the face at 120 miles per hour. The big raindrops feel like hypodermic needles stabbing them everywhere.

It's not long before Harker turns the team toward Cambodia, and then it's over the border for three klicks. Bagley is watching the map, the heading, and the clock, to help Harker with the navigation. Beam follows.

Bagley speaks first: "Okay, we've got about half a klick to go. Better slow us down."

"Gotcha," Harker says.

Beam sees the lead bird slowing down. "Okay, boys," he says over the ICS. "Get ready. We're fixing to dump our cargo." O.B. and Mack tell the SEALs they need to get in the ready position. Anderson, with his Stoner, and Eric, with his M-60, move onto the skid in front of Mack. Kennedy, with his M-203, and Oliver, with his M-60, move onto the skid in front of O.B.

Hollywood can see Benedict and Animal standing out on the skids of Harker's bird in front of them. He almost laughs because Animal holds Johnny with one hand by the scruff of his black pajamas and is dangling the kid out over nothingness.

"We have arrived," Bagley says.

With that, Harker flares and sinks his chopper into the tall elephant grass. As it cuts through the tall grass and just about comes to a stop, all four SEALs, with Johnny, disappear into the darkness.

The same thing is true for the SEALs on Beam's bird. Man, when they're gone, they're gone!

Harker pushes his bird and up he goes again, with Beam right on his tail. Staying low, the two Seawolf gunships head back across the border and turn south.

On the ground, Animal passes Johnny to Moloney. Taking up point, Animal moves quickly through the tall grass. At line-of-sight distance, Moloney is right on his heels, with Johnny in tow. Benedict is behind him, followed by Fritz, and so on, back to the rear guard, Eric.

It's only a klick until they reach the target canal. Then they'll set up the ambush.

As for the Seawolves—it doesn't take them long to reach the waiting spot. As the two gunships start to get close, Harker turns off all his lights and banks on Beam not flying up his ass in the terrible weather. Beam has great night vision, though. No problem.

Harker flares out and sets his bird down on a dike between rice paddies. It's a tedious landing because the skids slip around on the mud on top of the dike. Beam comes in and sets down behind him. Both birds shut down as fast as possible so as not to draw any attention. Both Harker and Beam are pulling on their rotor blade brakes like there's no tomorrow, to stop the rotors. The rain is still coming down like crazy.

Nimmo, being the oldest and most mature gunner—as the others sometimes joke—gets out with the Starlight Scope and checks the surrounding treelines for any movement.

All looks secure, so it's time to sit back and wait for the SEALs to call.

Back in Cambodia, the SEALs have just about reached their first objective—the canal that Johnny pointed out on the map at the meeting back at the outpost.

Animal moves the team from the tall grass into the jungle, which means the canal has to be very close. Moloney, with Johnny still in tow, sees Animal stop in his tracks. Jesus, he's thinking, this guy is like a pointer back home, bird hunting. When he stops, he stops. You can't even see him breathing.

Everyone else stops as well. They're waiting for Animal to give the all clear. And he does. He's found the canal, which is why he stopped.

Like a bunch of water snakes, they all slither into the canal and make their way to the other side. Once there, they spread out among the reeds, all of them up to their shoulders in the water. Their weapons are held up as if they're taking aim. They adjust to the tide so as not to give their position away if they're going to be there a while. Johnny is still by Moloney's side.

Benedict looks at his watch. They're right on schedule. It's twelve midnight. Eric is the assigned man to grab the tango. Anderson is to take Eric's spot as rear guard. Now all they have to do is wait.

Back in the rice paddy with the Seawolves, Nimmo makes the rounds with the Starlight Scope every few minutes to make sure all is still secure. The smoking lamp is definitely out. Otherwise it could be your last cigarette forever.

The Seawolves just sit there with their M-60s at the ready and stare into the rainy night with strained eyes. The copilots have their M-16s in their laps just in case. The pilots are focused on starting up as fast as possible in case they're discovered. And the rain just keeps coming down as if nothing else is going on. Mother Nature doesn't care.

Back at the canal, the SEALs are making themselves as uncomfortable as possible so they'll stay alert. That part is easy. If you've ever been in South Vietnam at night in the middle of the monsoon season with rain just pouring down, you'd know that it gets very cold. The water in the canal is warm, which would be nice if not for the critters swimming around, taking small bites out of the men.

It's closing in on 0200 hours when Animal gives a sign that he hears something. It's the faint sound of an outboard motor puttering along real slow, coming in their direction. Eric gets ready. All the guys are still, like the reeds they're hiding in. The rain is still coming down but it's let up a little.

A small sampan comes into view. Johnny gives the sign to Moloney that this is the guy, and Moloney passes the info on down the line to Eric, using hand signals. Eric is ready. The tango is definitely alone.

As he comes into Eric's view and Eric gets a good look at him, he sees that this is going to be a snap. He's a very small guy, and the little sampan is moving at about the same speed a trolling motor would move a bass boat back home.

He waits till the last possible second, when the little guy is directly parallel to him. Eric closes the distance between them in a microsecond, reaches up, and grabs him by his black pajama top. As he's pulling him over the side into the water, Eric's foot hits something slippery on the bottom of the canal and he loses his footing. He goes under, dragging his prisoner with him. Trying not to flail about in the water, which would make a lot of noise, he can't get his footing or find the surface.

Well, this is great, Eric is thinking. I got the prize and now I'm going to drown the little shit, and me along with him.

Oliver comes to the rescue, grabbing the man's hair under the water and pulling with all his might with one hand while holding his M-60 above the water with the other. This also helps stabilize Eric enough for Eric to regain his footing and recover from the embarrassing situation.

Kennedy moves in and gags the prisoner, while Eric quickly ties his hands behind his back. The package is ready to be moved.

Animal moves to the shore and takes point once again, leading the team farther south toward the extraction point. Benedict follows close behind with his CAR-15 at the ready, watching to the left. Moloney is next, watching to the right with his Stoner in one hand and Johnny in the other. Behind him is Fritz, watching to the left with his M-60. He's also keeping an eye on Johnny. Behind Fritz is Kennedy, with the radio, and he's watching to the right with his M-203.

Next is Eric and Oliver, with the prisoner between them. They both have M-60s, and Eric is watching the left, Oliver the right. It takes a strong man to carry a prisoner in one hand and an M-60 machine gun in the other. Anderson is watching 180 degrees behind them with his Stoner.

After they had put about one hundred paces between them and the canal, Benedict has the team stop while he calls Harker. Moving back to Kennedy, he pulls the telephone from the PRC-25 radio on his back and transmits in a whisper. "Seawolf, Seawolf, Scorpion One, Scorpion One. Do you copy? Over."

Back in the rice paddy three and a half klicks away, eight Seawolves jump as if shot out of a gun. Nimmo stashes the Starlight Scope, Harker and Beam hit the start-up trigger on their jet engines as Bagley hits his mike button. "Scorpion One, Scorpion One. This is Seawolf One-six. We copy. Over."

"Seawolf, Seawolf. Scorpion One. We have acquired package. I say again, we have acquired package. Will be ready for extraction as planned. Over."

Both birds are almost turning up now as Bagley hits

his mike button again. "Scorpion One. Seawolf One-six. We are en route. Over."

The rain is coming down lightly now as the SEAL squad starts moving again. What they don't know is that the people their prisoner was on his way to meet were worried when he didn't show up and went looking for him. They found an empty boat. And since this is Cambodia, and an area they know like the backs of their hands, it doesn't take them long to figure out where whoever grabbed their buddy is headed.

Animal just keeps moving on toward the extraction point. All the SEALs are keeping a good pace, considering they have Johnny and one prisoner to worry about.

Benedict has taken up his position behind Animal again after talking on the radio. And just about the time he gets settled in, Animal freezes again. Jesus Christ, this guy is creepy, Benedict is thinking. Of course, everyone else stops too.

Animal signals to Benedict that they better set up a defensive position. Something is coming their way in a big hurry, and he can't quite tell which direction they're coming from yet.

They're in the middle of a field of tall elephant grass, where someone would have to trip over them to find them, and suddenly a VC comes running out of the grass right in front of Benedict with an AK-47 pointing straight at him. Luckily for him, the SEAL Team leader is pointing his CAR-15 at the man and instinctively pulls the trigger. A long burst rings out over the field as the VC stumbles forward into Benedict's arms, dead.

At the same time, a VC runs square into Fritz, who's

carrying an M-60 and blows him straight back into the grass.

The same thing happens to Eric, and to the VC he shoots at, blowing him back into the grass.

Anderson, the rear guard, starts dropping VC behind them with his Stoner. That's all Animal needs to know. He decides that going forward would probably be best. So much for the defensive position plan. Now it's the run-like-hell plan. It doesn't take a Harvard graduate to tell them all that. The team instinctively moves into the leapfrog maneuver and they start making their way toward the extraction point.

Moloney isn't worrying about Johnny anymore; he's on his own. For his part, Johnny stays right with Moloney. He doesn't want to be left behind.

Eric and Oliver take the prisoner forward of the group. They know he has to be kept alive. He has important information.

As Anderson's Stoner runs out of ammo, Kennedy lays down cover fire so Anderson can move and reload. As Kennedy runs out of ammo and pops an M-79 grenade for good measure, he moves and reloads while Fritz lays down cover fire for him with his M-60. Next it's Moloney's turn to lay down cover fire while Fritz moves and reloads. Then it's Benedict's turn to lay down cover fire while Moloney moves and reloads. After Benedict, it's Anderson's turn again, and so on. Animal stays out front as point man, in case they run into another group that's trying to cut them off.

Now, as Animal moves forward with his CAR-15 in one hand and his K-bar knife in the other, a VC stumbles right in front of him. A quick three-round burst in the face dispatches the VC in rapid fashion.

Still moving forward, another VC comes out of the grass straight toward Animal. He looks up at Animal's skull-painted face and freezes just long enough for Animal to let go with another burst, which gets him in the face too, and drops him like a stone.

Animal is starting to think that things aren't looking real good. How many more of these guys are there to run into? Is the team fixing to walk straight into an ambush or what?

Back behind Animal, VC are now coming at them from the side again. If not for the quick thinking of Moloney and Kennedy, picking those few off, they'd have been fucked big-time. It all goes back to training, training, training. Always expect the unexpected and you'll live longer.

The sound of helicopters makes Animal pick up the tempo. Except it's a little different this time. It sounds like they're on the ground.

Animal stumbles into a clearing right in front of him. It's been made by two great big weed eaters. They're sitting side by side—the two Seawolf helicopter gunships. No lights on, just sitting there in the dark, waiting for the SEAL Team in the rain. Talk about navigation kings! Animal thinks.

O.B., Mack, Nimmo, and Buddy are standing outside on top of their respective rocket pods, taking aim with their M-60s, waiting on the SEALs to clear the firing line. As soon as they're all present and accounted for, the four Seawolves are going to cut loose with their M-60s.

As the SEALs stumble into the clearing, they have a noticeable, shocked look on their faces. Animal stays at the edge of the clearing as each teammate makes his way out of the tall grass, into the clearing, and into the choppers. Eric and Oliver, with the prisoner in tow, are the first onto Harker's bird. The rest, after emptying their weapons in cover fire, jump on board. Now it's the gunners' turn. Nimmo, Buddy, Mack, and O.B. spray the whole area down with their M-60s. The red and green tracers are flying everywhere as the two gunships rise up into a hover next to each other.

Then comes a big surprise for Charlie. Both gunships start punching off all twenty-eight rockets, completely blanketing the area with high explosive and white phosphorus warheads. Even with all the rain, they start fires in the elephant grass, which sets up a smoke screen nobody can see through.

At the same time, both birds do an about-face and take off in the direction of the border.

As they go back up to the safe altitude of 25 feet, Eric looks over at Animal and notices blood running down both of his arms. "Jesus Christ, Animal," he says. "You've got little cuts all over both your arms, man. It was that damn elephant grass." Eric pauses as he looks at Animal's face, and decides not to continue.

Animal just looks back at him as if to say, "And your point?"

Mission accomplished, without casualties.

23

The day before the Vietnamese New Year celebration of Tet in 1968, Lieutenant Commander Jack Bolton called a meeting in the officers' quarters at Nha Be. All the officers were present at the briefing, which Lieutenant Richard Benedict of SEAL Team One was giving. The meeting consisted of a report on the latest intelligence that had been gathered by the teams, with the assistance of the Seawolves and River Rats.

"Gentlemen," Benedict said, "we've come to the conclusion that Charlie has been building up for something really big on the horizon. All the signs point toward an all-out offensive here in the South. I think it's going to happen very soon. It has been reported to the powers that be, and the answer we're getting back is that it won't happen until the 'Tet cease-fire' is over. Even then, they say, it's unlikely to be as big as we're telling them."

"That's correct," Bolton said. "As usual, we've been ordered to stand down along with the rest of the U.S. forces in honor of the agreement signed by both sides so as not to disturb the Tet celebration in North and South Vietnam. We're not too surprised that they're taking our warning with a grain of salt."

"How big is this offensive expected to be?" Lieutenant (j.g.) John Luscher asked.

"Well," Benedict replied, "I'd say every major base and city, including Cam Ranh Bay, Da Nang, and Saigon, south of the DMZ and covering the entire country, is going to get the shit kicked out of 'em!"

"Damn, that's going to be nuts!" said Pistol Boswell, who was now back at Det. Two.

Bolton went on to say, "We all need to get as much rest as possible during this 'stand down' time, just in case all this is true. So don't plan on doing a whole lot of partying. Stay sober, and make sure your men do as well. Remember, the Tet celebration starts at midnight tonight."

Everyone left the meeting disappointed because they were all looking forward to that time to unwind from the daily drudgery of the war. They also knew that what had been discussed was very serious and that they all needed to get a lot of rest—rest today so they could party at a later date.

The word was passed, and everyone spent the rest of the day cleaning guns and pulling maintenance inspections on the helicopters.

That night, the entire country went to sleep after spending the day gearing down for the holiday to come. From Binh Thuy to Vinh Long, from Dong Tam to Vung Tau, all was shut down in preparation for the holiday to begin.

To the south of Saigon there was an outpost manned by the U.S. 9th Infantry. Their call sign was "Digger One." To the north of Saigon another outpost manned by the 9th Infantry Division was called "Digger Two." Both were shut down for the night, as was an outpost manned by a Green Beret Mike Force just north of Tan Son Nhut Air Force Base, call sign "Striker King." No patrols being pulled at all that night.

The headquarters for the U.S. 199th Light Infantry Brigade, along with the StarCom-Satellite Communications Center, were tucked in for the coming holiday. The same was true for the Main U.S. PX and Commissary, the National Assembly building, U.S. Aid Headquarters, the USIS building, the prime minister's office building and compound, the main government office building, and the U.S. Embassy.

At Main U.S. Military Headquarters, everyone had retired for the night or was at the base club getting smashed. The last thing they had to worry about was an offensive. They were completely safe in Saigon, they assumed, so why worry about how much they had to drink?

The President's Palace was silent. The palace guards were relaxed, ready for Tet to begin. This was fun time for all and no worries.

Jack Bolton, John Luscher, Dick Stout, and Pistol Boswell were all sleeping soundly. George "Sappy" Sappenfield, Terry Reasoner, Tim Brooks, Bob Erickson, and the rest of the gunners were out after a long hot day of cleaning and fixing things. First Class Petty Officer Erickson, a jet mechanic, was the enlisted man in charge of the aircrew. He was one of those guys that had a hot rod in the fifties and had his own car club. Hollywood, California, was glad to see him go into the Navy—it made things a lot quieter around town.

• • •

Bells going off rudely interrupted the restful slumber. Adding insult to injury, everyone heard a screaming voice over the loudspeaker saying, "Scramble the helos, scramble the helos, scramble one, scramble one!"

All the pilots in the officers' quarters stirred. Bolton mumbled out to the rest, "What kind of fucking sick joke is that anyway?"

To which Luscher answered, "I don't know, but if we ever find out who, let's hang him up by his balls."

Pistol asked, "What time is it anyway?"

Stout answered, "Jesus Christ, it's 0130," which meant one-thirty in the morning. And with that they all rolled over and went back to sleep.

About two minutes later the loudspeaker went off again: "Scramble the helos, scramble the helos, scramble one, this is not a drill, scramble one! Saigon is under heavy attack! Scramble one!"

This time the men did more than merely stir. They hit the floor in complete shock. Bolton jumped in his flight suit, Luscher already had his cutoffs on and just threw on his T-shirt, and Stout and Pistol had their tiger stripes on and were hitting the door.

All the gunners were already at the birds, getting them ready for flight. Sappy was putting down the contacts on the rocket pods and locking the barrels in the flex guns, while Reasoner was unhooking the main rotor blade from the tail boom and walking it around front. Erickson and Brooks were doing the same to their bird.

Luscher, Stout, Pistol, and Bolton ran across from the Quonset huts toward their revetments and their waiting choppers. They slowed to a walk as Bolton said, "What the fuck?"

Luscher said, "What kind of shit is this?" as all four naval officers looked around at the night sky. It was as peaceful as a spring night in the Georgia countryside. So where was the war?

They were all puzzled because nothing was happening in the area of Nha Be. They didn't see or hear any gunfire or mortars going off at all and suspected that this might still be some kind of sick joke. If Saigon was getting overrun, why wasn't their base hit as well?

Nevertheless, the scramble continued. Reasoner was holding on to his rotor blade, as was Erickson. Brooks and Sappy were in their respective positions with M-60s in their laps. Luscher and Bolton, almost at the same time, yelled out, "Clear! Coming hot!" And the jet engines of each helicopter started to whine. Stout in his copilot seat and Pistol in his tuned in their respective radios. They could hear people screaming for help. It sounded like men were being killed in their beds in all the barracks located all over Saigon. Among the garbled communications, because everyone was walking on everyone else, it seemed that a massive North Vietnamese Army (NVA) force had hit just about every base in the city. Enemy troops were running all over the streets freely.

Luscher was thinking, My God, if that's true, our boys are in big trouble! He thought as much because everything was thought to be completely safe in Saigon, to the point where weapons were not needed. On top of that, no one knew where to go to get any in case of an emergency.

The only people authorized to pack a gun in Saigon were the MPs (Army Military Police), the SPs (Navy Shore Patrol), the APs (U.S. Air Force Police), the

Marines guarding the Annapolis Hotel and the American embassy, and the South Vietnamese police. That was it.

And now it sounded as if thousands of North Vietnamese regulars, armed to the teeth, were hitting all of Saigon and all its military locations at once. The only resistance they had to worry about was a handful of jeeps with .50 caliber machine guns mounted in back and a scattering of M-16s here and there throughout the city. As far as base security went, the sense of feeling totally secure had bred complacency, which in turn had bred low or no security.

The rotor blades were pulled from Erickson's and Reasoner's hands. They ran back and mounted up in their positions, put their helmets on, and locked the barrels in the M-60s on their laps. Giving the all clear, Luscher and Bolton pulled up into a hover. Moving sideways out of their revetments, they lined up one behind the other on the short dirt runway. As Stout and Pistol were taking notes on what was going on over the radio, their pilots pushed the gunships forward, accelerating toward the river. Up and away they went into the dark sky.

Meanwhile, the SEAL Team had been donning their gear, getting ready for combat. Lieutenant Benedict was not too surprised by the scramble. All that he'd heard the last several weeks pointed to it, but he hadn't been able to get anyone to listen to reason. After all, Naval Intelligence could only do so much. It looked like he and his fifteen guys were in for a crazy time of hunting and killing.

By the time Bolton and his team took off, Benedict and his men were making their way down to the boat dock. They were going to split up into three LSSCs and head up to Saigon to see what kind of shit they could stir up.

Climbing up to altitude, the Seawolves saw a horrifying sight. All of Saigon was spread out before them, and it was a fireworks display to end all fireworks displays. Flashes of exploding mortars and rockets were hitting targets by the hundreds all over. Red and green tracers shot through the sky like so many fireflies in the country on a summer night.

The radio on all frequencies was jammed with panicking people yelling for help.

One other thing the crews noticed, or rather, didn't notice. There were no other aircraft anywhere in the sky over Saigon. Either that, or they were all flying without lights, which just wasn't done. This airspace was usually filled with air traffic, and if you didn't fly with any running lights at all, you'd fly into someone.

Bolton, in Seawolf 26, was flying lead. Luscher, in Seawolf 24, was flying the trail bird. They had never been trained for urban combat. All they knew was jungle warfare. This would be a whole new ball game for them.

The radio came alive on a strong frequency that walked on all the others. It was "Moon River," the call sign for the Seawolf base at Nha Be.

"Seawolf Two-six, Seawolf Two-six, Moon River, Moon River, do you copy? Over."

"Moon River, Seawolf Two-six. Go ahead. Over."

"Seawolf Two-six, Moon River. We have Annapolis Hotel on the line. They have multiple targets. Can you assist? Over."

"Moon River, Seawolf Two-six, we copy. Have them come up on our push. Over."

"Roger that, Two-six, we copy. Moon River out."

Luscher was wondering how they were going to find them in the dark and with all the explosions going off.

"Seawolf Two-six, Annapolis One, do you copy? Over."

"Annapolis One, Seawolf Two-six, I copy. Over."

"Seawolf, what's your ETA my location? Over."

"Annapolis One, Seawolf Two-six. As best as I can tell ETA your location about twelve mikes. Do you copy? Over."

"Roger that, Seawolf. We need you to pop flares over our location so we can see targets. Can you do that? Over."

"Annapolis One, Seawolf Two-six. Can do. Also, where do you want us to strike? Over."

"Seawolf! Everywhere! Anywhere! We're getting the shit shot out of us by some big guns but we can't tell where they're coming from! Over!"

Damn, he sounds scared shitless, Bolton thought. Then he answered, "Annapolis One, Seawolf Two-six. Don't worry. We're almost there. Hang on, Annapolis One."

"Roger that, Seawolf!"

Coming over the city at 1,000 feet in the middle of the night with the explosions and gunfire all over was going to make it hard to find their way. Luckily, Bolton had an incredible sense of direction. He could see the lights at Tan Son Nhut, and using that as a reference point, he slowly led the team right over the Annapolis Hotel.

Both gunships saw large tracers bouncing way up in the sky much higher than they were flying. They assumed the tracers were coming from the heavy guns Annapolis One had been talking about. They had to be .50 caliber. The Seawolves knew they would have to be very careful of those guns, which could shoot down jet planes, not to mention helicopters.

"Two-four, Two-six," Bolton said.

"Two-six, Two-four," Luscher answered.

"Two-four, Two-six. You see those tracers?"

"Roger that," Luscher answered.

"We gotta be careful of those guns. See if you can spot where they're coming from!"

"Will do," Luscher answered.

"Two-four, Two-six," Bolton said. "Brooks and Erickson are going to pop flares. Feel free to let Sappy and Terry take any targets of opportunity. Over."

"Roger that, Two-six."

Luscher was flying blacked out and lower than Bolton. That way, they could get a better view of the streets below when the flares started going off. Also, it would make it easier for Sappy and Terry Reasoner to take out tangos.

"Okay, boys, here we go," Luscher said. "Keep an eye open for those big guns!"

As soon as the first flare lit up the hotel and all the surrounding streets and buildings, Sappy and Terry started dropping Charlies all over the place. It was like a turkey shoot. The tangos were all over the streets down below, running from one building to another. The green tracers made it even easier to tell friends from foes. Another thing that made it easy was that there weren't that many friends around, not when the people on the ground were shooting up at them.

After the first pass over the hotel, Dick Stout, Luscher's copilot, spotted a building across the street that had some seriously large muzzle flashes coming out of two windows, both on the same floor. Four or five windows separated those two. He passed the information on to Bolton, who jumped on the radio.

"Annapolis One, Seawolf Two-six. We have large flashes coming from the building south of you. Do you copy?"

"Seawolf, Seawolf, *no shit!* That's gotta be the ones that are keeping our heads down most of the time! Over!"

"Roger that, Annapolis One," Bolton answered. "We copy! It'll just take a minute and we'll have those guns taken care of. Over."

He knew that those guns had to be giving the Marine guards a real hard time.

Bolton brought the team back around, dropped down low, and lined up for a run. Brooks and Erickson stopped popping flares and got in position, ready to hit the target building once their boss gave them the signal to open up with their M-60s.

"Two-four, Two-six. We're going in low over the tops of the buildings. Just follow me. Two darts with a left break. Over."

"Roger, Two-six. In low, two darts with a break left."

The only way to approach big guns like that with a helicopter was to go as low as they could and surprise them.

This is going to be a kick-ass ride, Sappy was thinking. Making a run on a building!

Bolton made his approach right on the rooftops. It was tricky flying that low at night. A pilot had to have very good night vision to dodge the rooftops, each of which was at a different altitude. Bobbing and dodging up and down, in and out, Bolton lined up his rocket sight as best he could on one of the windows that had the .50 caliber in it. He was basically guessing where it was because he wouldn't be able to see it until just before he was ready to shoot. Hopefully, all the surrounding buildings and activity would disguise what they were about to do.

Luscher was coming in just to the right of his lead bird and about 100 yards back. Bolton had the top red light on his bird going so Luscher could see where he was. Luscher was also having a hard time keeping his bird out of any entanglements, given the varying heights of the rooftops as he made his approach. And he also had to guesstimate the exact location of his target window.

Pistol, Bolton's copilot, was lining up his flex gun sights and holding off to the last minute so as not to give their position away. Bright red tracers coming from their chopper and headed for the target would be a dead giveaway.

In addition, the lead bird's top red light not only told Luscher where it was but made it a good target for the NVAs still running around the streets. They could only pray that it wouldn't draw too much attention as it zipped past the alleys between the buildings below. Or at least not until it was too late.

Bolton was almost right on top of the Annapolis Hotel when he popped up to about 100 feet and let his two HE rockets fly. Pistol opened up with his flex guns and covered the whole side of the target building, exploding little holes of concrete and dust to shower down on the street below. Erickson and Brooks were doing the same. Glass was breaking everywhere as the .308s ripped through the windows on all the floors.

Bolton made a hard turn just as the rockets impacted the target window, one right behind the other. He came close to flying through the blast of his own exploding rockets.

Sappy and Terry were leaning way outside and firing their M-60s like crazy, trying to give Bolton as much cover as feasibly possible. There was a VC sniper on the rooftop of another building who Sappy saw shooting at Bolton's bird. About two seconds later Sappy had put that sniper on a permanent vacation.

The secret was out. Everyone knew the Seawolves had arrived on the scene. The Seawolves could tell from the hits they were now taking in the tail boom. An AK-47 round tearing through aircraft aluminum sounds like someone hitting it with a baseball bat.

The tail boom was getting hit because they were flying low and fast, which usually throws the enemy off when they try to lead you in their sights. So, when Luscher's bird was taking hits, he knew that Bolton was getting it just as bad, if not worse.

Seeing Bolton escaping to the left, Luscher punched his missiles off, sending them straight through the other window. They exploded inside of the building. Excited, Reasoner hit his ICS button while he kept shooting his M-60 as Luscher broke off his run to the left. "Jesus Christ," he said, "I saw a body blow straight out of the window and fall to the street below! Damn nice shooting!"

Exiting the area, the two gunships were still taking fire from the streets below. Bolton had the team climb back up to 1,000 feet.

The guys down at the Annapolis Hotel called and said thanks. The run evidently stopped the onslaught, for the moment anyway. It gave the team a little breather and enough time to realize again that they still seemed to be the only gunships in the air over the whole city, which was puzzling.

Another panicky call came over the radio: "Seawolf, Seawolf, Alpha Bravo Two, Alpha Bravo Two. Over."

"Alpha Bravo Two, Seawolf Two-six, go ahead. Over."

"Seawolf, Seawolf, Alpha Bravo Two. We need your help over here at the Main Uniform Sierra Mike Headquarters, ASAP. Over." The Main U.S. Military Headquarters was a large base containing a lot of office buildings and barracks.

"Alpha Bravo Two, Seawolf Two-six. Roger. We are en route. Over."

Luscher and Bolton could barely filter out the distress calls because everyone was still walking on each other over the airwaves. And all of them were calling Seawolf in a panic.

It doesn't take long to get someplace when you're flying. If you had to drive from one spot to another, well, that's a whole different story. Anyway, once there, it was a matter of deciding which of the dozen targets to hit within the base. Alpha Bravo Two said there had been a lot of U.S. killed while sleeping in their beds. Once everyone was awake, it became a slaughter; a bloodbath, if you will. That was because no one on the base had any guns. Most of the MPs had been killed because they were so outnumbered.

However, the Chinese Communist green tracers were like a map in the night for locating the NVA. All four of the Seawolf gunners were free-firing at all targets of opportunity as the team flew over the base at 800 feet.

Alpha Bravo Two was at the main communications building and was under heavy attack from all sides. Those who were left of the MPs were trying to fight them off, but they were running out of ammunition. Once Bolton had zeroed in on Alpha Bravo Two's exact location, he lined up the team for a run.

"Two-four, Two-six. You hit the east and near side and I'll hit the far and west side. Six darts with a right break. You copy?"

"Two-six, Two-four. I hit east and near side, six darts with a break right. Roger."

That would cover all sides with one run. This would take a standard run too. It was the only way Bolton and Luscher could get a good enough spread with their rockets on the target. They started the run at 800 feet going down to 400 feet before they broke off the attack. That way they got a good angle on the target and would also be able to get in close.

Down they went, Bolton leading the charge. Pistol, Erickson, and Brooks were giving the NVA in the surrounding buildings hell. All the green tracers that had been going into the communications building were now coming up at the two Seawolf gunships.

Bolton lined up and punched off three rockets, sending them into the buildings west of Alpha Bravo Two's location. Two of those were high explosive and the third was a white phosphorus. Just as they found their marks and started exploding, he punched off three more missiles into the buildings on the far side, two of them white phosphorus and one high explosive. Three more explosions silenced more green tracers. Bolton broke off his attack to the right as Brooks and Erickson cleaned up the streets all around. The WP rockets were starting some serious fires in the buildings, which helped the good guys because of all the light they were putting off, and because the NVAs were now running around the street on fire.

Luscher's first three rockets tore through the buildings on the near side, then three more exploded in the buildings to the east. They were the same spread of HE and WP rockets as Bolton's and had the same effect. Fires popped up everywhere, and there were more burning NVA soldiers in the street.

A green enemy tracer flew through Luscher's cockpit. It came in one side and out the other without hitting anything. It was the size of a basketball. As a pucker inducer, it went clear off the scale.

Bolton led the team back up to 800 feet and flew over the base with Erickson and Brooks in the back popping flares again, and Luscher's guys cleaning up on the NVAs below. Another turkey shoot.

Erickson and Brooks were starting to complain. They wanted their turn. Since Sappy and Terry were getting low on ammunition anyway, Bolton said, "Two-four, Two-six. I'm going to come around on your six. Let Sappy and Terry pop flares."

"Roger that, Two-six. I copy."

With that, Luscher climbed up to 1,000 feet and turned on his red flashing light on top so 26 could see where he was. Bolton turned his red flashing light off as he broke off from the lead and started his turn to come back behind Luscher. He came around on to 24's six o'clock position and leveled off at 600 feet. Erickson and Brooks were ready with their M-60s, just waiting for the first flare to light up on its parachute.

When it went off, Erickson and Brooks were excited. The pop flares lit things up like mid-afternoon sunlight, revealing tangos everywhere to kill.

Their M-60s came alive, taking out NVAs everywhere. The two gunners were amazed at the number they were killing. It told them what a nightmare it must have been for those people in the barracks on this base and so many others around the city.

After running up the score for a while, a couple of APCs came driving through the main gate with .30 caliber machine guns working out. Reinforcements had arrived. It wasn't much, but it was enough to handle the continued rescue of Alpha Bravo Two and the MPs who were left, and the APCs were also bringing more ammunition for those remaining MPs.

Besides, more people were calling for the Seawolves to come and help them out, so it was time to move on.

"Alpha Bravo Two, Seawolf Two-six. Are you secure? Over."

"Roger that, Seawolf! Thanks a lot for your help!"

As the last parachuting flare slowly burned itself out in the dark sky, and Bolton's gunners temporarily ran out of targets, the radio came alive with another strong signal walking on the others.

"Seawolf, Seawolf, Alpha Bravo One-two, Alpha Bravo One-two. Do you copy? Over." The call was from U.S. Aid Headquarters.

"Alpha Bravo One-two, this is Seawolf Two-six. We copy. Over."

"Seawolf, Seawolf, Alpha Bravo One-two. We need *help!* What's your ETA? Over."

"Alpha Bravo One-two, Seawolf Two-six. ETA two mikes. Over."

"Roger that, Seawolf. We've got Charlies out the ass over here!"

"We copy, Alpha Bravo One-two. Where do you want it? Over."

"On the wall out front, Seawolf. *They're coming over the wall!*"

"*Roger that!*" Bolton answered.

Two Vietnamese police with M-1s, and four U.S. Army guards with M-16s, had lost their hold on the wall and had to retreat into the building. They were firing out the windows at the VC who were climbing over the top of the wall surrounding the front yard. The defenders did have two .30 caliber machine guns, one on each corner out front, but they'd run out of ammunition. Because of the sheer number of VC charging them from the street, they had to grab up their machine guns and move inside to avoid hand-to-hand combat.

Bolton retook the lead and brought the fire team down to low level to make their upcoming run. The incoming fire on their two gunships was getting heavier all the time. Flying their rocket runs low level seemed to give them a little breathing room.

The U.S. Aid Headquarters building was on a main thoroughfare that was long and straight, which also made it easy to find. They just had to follow the streetlights.

Down they went, below the tops of the buildings on either side, guns blazing. As they passed cross streets, the gunners were picking off VC and NVA with their M-60s. Pistol had already opened up with his flex guns, taking out men who were running around in the middle of the street in front of them.

Bolton got on the radio. "Once we get an eye on the target," he said, "make it three darts break left."

"Roger that, Two-six! Three darts left-hand break," Luscher said.

They saw it on the right-hand side of the street. They were coming up on it fast.

"Alpha Bravo One-two, this is Seawolf Two-six. *Duck!*" Bolton said.

He could see all the VC in the street and on the wall. He was thinking, Damn, it's as if the movies just let out and they're all rushing for the parking lot. How about a sneak preview, boys? And with that he squeezed off three rockets, one after the other.

The sparks flew in the cockpit as they exited their tubes. A shower of red tracers from six M-60s followed the white blast coming from the rocket engines straight out in front of the Seawolf helicopter.

The first dart, a WP rocket, exploded in the middle of the crowd in the street out front, setting a couple dozen guys on fire. The next dart, an HE rocket, hit the top of the wall. The third one, another HE, also exploded on top of the wall. Several hundred red tracers were bouncing off the concrete and flying skyward as they tore through bodies. And there were four other rounds in between the tracer rounds.

The two Vietnamese police and the four Army guys who were shooting from the windows were rolled back into the middle of the reception area from the shock wave of the blasts. Just a few pieces of shrapnel and chunks of the wall made it through the windows. They ducked just in time for it to go over their heads.

Luscher hit his transmit button and said, "Alpha Bravo One-two, this is Seawolf Two-four. Stay down! Over!" And with that, Luscher's three rockets started impacting the wall as well. Bolton had just broken off his run, rolling up and to the left, flying clear of the surrounding buildings.

Sappy and Terry were dismembering men everywhere as Luscher's last rocket pounded the wall. Bodies were being blown up and into the side of the building, then falling into the front yard lifeless and in pieces. Some of the body parts were getting blown clear back across the street. Those who were still alive scattered like cockroaches after a porch light had been turned on. Half of the fleeing men were running around in circles, engulfed in flames.

Bolton took the team back up to 1,000 feet and had Luscher take the front door and pop flares over the top of Alpha Bravo 12's location.

Erickson and Brooks did the mop-up as the guys in the U.S. Aid Headquarters called in their thanks to the Seawolf gunships.

Bolton's idea of coming down the street as he did had surprised the enemy. Neither bird had taken any rounds.

24

On the radio there were still appeals for help, but the Seawolves were too low on fuel and ammunition. So they headed for the 9th Infantry outpost, Digger One. U.S. Army gunships were stationed at that location, which meant they had the fuel, rockets, and ammunition the Seawolves desperately needed.

"Say, boss," Erickson said over his ICS, "I see a jeep with a .50 caliber and an APC in the middle of this intersection straight under us that are firing like mad at the surrounding buildings. What do ya say we drop our last three rockets and help these guys out?"

"Sounds great!" Bolton said.

"Two-four, Two-six. Do you see the jeep and the APC in the middle of this lit-up intersection below us?"

"Two-six, Two-four. Roger that!"

"Two-Four, Two-six. Let's bring it around and air mail our last three rockets into those buildings and help out our MPs down there."

"Roger that, Two-six!"

"Follow me down, Two-four. You take the near buildings and I'll take the far buildings. Break left. You copy?"

"I copy, Two-six. Left break and I take the near buildings."

Down they went, with Bolton taking them in low and fast. His gunship made a tight right-hand turn and dropped out of the sky like a rock. It was all Luscher could do to stay on his tail. Bolton brought his bird down to 100 feet and pulled up, leveling her out with such force that Erickson and Brooks could hardly lift the machine guns out of their laps. Luscher came right down with him on his six.

Bolton hadn't even bothered to call it in, he just acted. He had a clean shot right down the street at the jeep and the APC. It was easy to see where the enemy was because of the green tracers. As Pistol opened up with the flex guns and Erickson and Brooks cut loose, they saw that the .50 caliber on the back of the jeep and the .30 caliber on the top of the APC had stopped shooting. The MPs couldn't help but notice something was going on, with hundreds of tracers coming out of the dark sky, seemingly from nowhere. The walls of the buildings at the far side of the intersection just lit up with hundreds of bullet holes and with exploding plaster tossed to the street below.

Bolton launched his three rockets. The first one, a WP, hit the third floor of the building to the left, setting it on fire. The second, another WP, hit the second floor of the other building, setting it on fire as well. Bolton's third and last was an HE. It also hit the building to the right, exploding on the roof and blowing some VC to the street below. He broke off his attack as Erickson and Brooks covered their exit.

Luscher was right on target and hit the near buildings with the same mixture. The green tracers that were showering down on the MPs in the middle of the intersection had disappeared.

"Seawolf, Seawolf. This is Mickey Mouse, Mickey

Mouse. Thanks a bunch for the help! You guys scared the shit out of us! And we didn't mind at all!"

"Roger that, Mickey Mouse! We aim to please! Seawolf Two-six, out!"

One more small part of the city had been taken care of.

Bolton hit his mike button as he led the team back up to 1,000 feet, "Digger One, Digger One, Seawolf Two-six. Do you copy? Over."

There was a pause, so Bolton hit it again. "Digger One, Digger One, Seawolf Two-six, Seawolf Two-six. Do you copy? Over."

"Seawolf, Seawolf, this is Digger One, Digger One. We copy. Over."

"Digger One, Seawolf Two-six. We need a quick turnaround on everything. Can you assist? Over."

"Roger that, Seawolf. What's your ETA? Over."

"Digger One, Seawolf Two-six. ETA ten mikes. Do you copy?"

"Roger that, Seawolf. ETA ten mikes. You are clear to land at your discretion. Watch for debris on the runway. Other than that, we're ready for ya. Over."

As the team got closer, it was evident that the little base had been hit hard. Fires were burning everywhere, which at least made it easy to see where to land.

Bolton brought his bird in fast. Just before he thought the skids were going to hit the ground too hard, he rolled on his power and at the same time pulled the stick straight back. The rotor blades popped loudly as they grabbed a bigger and bigger chunk of the air, causing the helicopter to flare gracefully, come to a stop, and ever so gently park the skids to rest on the dirt runway.

Luscher was right on his tail coming in, kicking up dust as his chopper came to a gentle rest on the ground behind Bolton.

The U.S. Army ground crews were ready and waiting with rockets, ammunition for the hungry M-60 machine guns, and all the fuel that the two UH1-Bs could hold. The gunners had just barely cleared their seats to get out and help the crews when rockets were being slid into the empty tubes. A fuel man was pumping JP-4 into the fuel cells, and two others had armfuls of belted .308 caliber bullets ready to reload the flex guns and door boxes.

Luscher, Stout, Bolton, and Pistol just sat in their seats, staring down the dirt flight line. What they saw made them sick. Helicopter after helicopter, gunship after gunship, were burning pieces of twisted metal. Some were still in their revetments, and some were out in the middle of the dirt runway. Undoubtedly they had been hit trying to scramble.

For some, the date December 7, 1941, must have come to mind. It would have reminded them of Pearl Harbor, perhaps because it had occurred during the Tet cease-fire agreement signed by both sides. Everyone had to shake it off, though. The birds were ready to hit it again. Erickson and Brooks cleared both sides and Bolton was up in hover check.

Sappy hit his ICS button. "Clear left."

Terry hit his ICS button. "Clear right."

Luscher pulled power, bringing his bird up to hover check.

Stout, Pistol, Erickson, Brooks, Sappy, and Terry popped smart salutes to the Army ground crews that were standing around, having just done a fabulous job under incredibly bad circumstances. They returned the salutes, and the Seawolves were off and running again.

As the two gunships disappeared into the dark night sky, the Army ground crews continued the work of separating their dead friends' bodies from the wreckage that seemed to be everywhere.

Back up to speed at 800 feet, Bolton was trying to distinguish between all the panicky calls on the radio. Everyone was still asking for the Seawolves. He had to grab hold of one that was understandable and had priority. It wasn't an easy task. Then one popped out above all the others.

"Seawolf, Seawolf, this is Sky Cap, Sky Cap. Do you copy? Over."

Sky Cap was the StarCom Satellite Communications Center. If Charlie got hold of that, he'd have a feather in his cap. It sounded like an enlisted communications man on the radio who was extremely scared.

"Sky Cap, Seawolf Two-six," Bolton replied. "We copy. Over."

"Seawolf, this is Sky Cap. We can't hold on much longer. The numbers are too great. *Help us out, man!*"

"Roger that, Sky Cap! We are en route! ETA five mikes. Hold on. Over."

As they closed in on Sky Cap's location, Bolton decided to stay at altitude and pop flares so Luscher and his crew could get a good look at the situation below. Then they would plan their attack run.

The parachute flares again lit up the complex like it was mid-afternoon, and they saw why the communications man had been so upset. It seemed as if somebody had kicked a fire ant hill in the middle of July. NVAs were swarming over the entire area.

Sappy and Terry didn't have to be told what to do. Their M-60s came alive, singing their favorite tune of "Let's Kill Charlie." Another turkey shoot was in progress as Luscher leveled off at 700 feet. He passed the bad news to Bolton. More bad guys to kill and more good guys to save. This was starting to get monotonous.

While Sappy and Terry continued firing, Bolton started to bring the choppers around for a rocket run. Once the last of the flares burned themselves out, Sappy and Terry stopped shooting.

The two Seawolf gunships rolled around and came in fast and hard. "Two-four, Two-six, three darts, break right."

"Roger that, three darts, right-hand break."

Down they went on a short and steep run from 800 feet. Bolton picked his shots fast and squeezed off three rockets one after the other. They all exploded into a main group of enemy soldiers and blasted bodies skyward. All three rockets were HE.

Pistol's flex guns, along with Erickson's and Brooks's M-60s, were scattering NVAs all over the complex.

As Bolton broke off his attack, Luscher could see where he'd sent his rockets and looked for the next available group that was packed together. He spotted just what he was looking for—a group huddled up, charging one of the gates at the near side of the complex. Zeroing his sights in just short of the gate, he let three HE rockets fly from their tubes.

His timing was perfect. Just as the group reached the gate, three large high-explosive warheads hit. The group attacking disappeared in a series of explosions. What was left of the advancing NVAs scattered in all directions, and Sappy and Terry, along with Stout and his flex guns, finishing the job with their pounding M-60 machine-gun fire.

Luscher broke off his attack and came around behind Bolton.

Sappy notified his pilot that he could see the NVAs starting to back off from the communications center.

Terry was busy counting his blessings, because two rounds had come up through the floor between his feet. They continued on up and out the rooftop of the helicopter.

Bolton came back around for another hit. "Three darts, break right," he barked out over the radio.

"Roger, three darts, right break," Luscher barked back.

Down they went again. Bolton had them pulling a tight daisy chain on this one. He wanted to kick ass and move on as fast as possible. He figured that if he did it this way, Charlie might think there were more than just two choppers.

As he brought his bird in line with the target, it looked as if the attack was letting up, just as Sappy had said. There weren't as many tracers bouncing around as before. Rapidly closing the distance on the enemy attackers, he could see two main groups left at the edge of the complex. Bolton concentrated on one and Luscher on the other.

Seawolf 26 came in fast again. Pistol was firing his flex guns like there was no tomorrow. Erickson and Brooks were dropping NVAs one at a time. They all had a lot of tracers coming back up at them again.

Bolton squeezed off three more after he picked out his next target area. The first two were white phosphorus. The last one was HE. More flaming bodies bounced around the ground as he broke off his run.

Erickson and Brooks were losing some of their night vision as tracers started cooking off in their white-hot barrels because they hadn't been able to change them.

Luscher, as usual, was on the money, his WP and HE finding their marks. More flaming bodies and body parts were left behind as he broke off from his run.

That enlisted communications man on the ground was a little less hyper now. "Seawolf, Seawolf, this is Sky Cap, Sky Cap. Thanks a bunch, guys! I think we got it from here. Thanks a lot!"

"Sky Cap, Seawolf Two-six. It's our pleasure. We be gone!" Bolton said.

It was time to continue on to the next fire that needed to be put out. And was it a fire!

Over the radio blasted, "Seawolf, Seawolf. Alpha Bravo Three, Alpha Bravo Three. Do you copy? Over!"

Bolton knew it was the American embassy. "Alpha Bravo Three, this is Seawolf Two-six," he responded. "We copy! Over!"

"Seawolf, Seawolf, we need help. We have two Australian medevac helicopters inbound and are taking too much fire for them to land. Can you cover? Over."

"Roger that. We are en route to your location. ETA ten mikes. Over."

The sun was just starting to peek over the horizon, to give the madness some daylight. If anything, it made the situation worse. Now everyone could see the Seawolf choppers overhead. Now everyone would be shooting at them.

The way Air Medals are earned in the U.S. Navy is on a point system: one point if you put in a strike on a known enemy position, half a point for flying a combat patrol, two points if you receive enemy fire, meaning you're shot at. A total of twenty points earned one Air Medal. On any given mission, the most you could get, according to regulations, was two points. Therefore, the Seawolves were getting a total of two points for getting shot at a total of five hours to that point. Reflecting upon it, it didn't seem fair at all to the men.

Arriving over the American embassy, the two gunships started receiving all kinds of fire. The gunners didn't even bother tossing out smoke grenades to try and spot who was shooting at them—the incoming rounds were from too many directions. They just started shooting at any targets of opportunity they could locate with their busy eyes.

Luscher was the first to spot the medevac approaching from the north. "Two-six, Two-four. I have our medevac at our one o'clock position. Over."

"Two-four, Two-six. Roger. We've got him."

There were buildings on either side and in the back of the embassy compound. Across the street from the front of the compound there was a golf course. The Seawolves were receiving fire from the surrounding buildings, but the bulk of it was coming from the golf course.

As the two gunships cruised at 800 feet over the embassy building below, Sappy hit his mike button while firing his M-60 and said, "Receiving fifty fire, receiving fifty fire!"

Almost at the same instant Bolton transmitted, "Receiving fifty fire, Two-four, we're receiving fifty fire!"

"Roger!" Luscher came back.

Both chopper pilots instinctively dropped their collectives and their birds fell out of the sky like rocks. They had to get down to treetop level, or rather, street top level, as soon as possible.

Seawolf 26 rolled the power back on and pulled up on the collective, leveling off the chopper and picking up speed as it moved down one of the streets next to the golf course. Luscher was right behind. They made it without getting shot down.

Both birds were screaming down the street between the buildings, dodging power lines as they went. The team had to work its way around and back to the embassy in order to give the medevac chopper the cover it was going to need. That .50 caliber gun had to go.

The two helicopter gunships flew below the tops of the buildings in downtown Saigon, making gut-wrenching turns at one intersection after the other. Bolton had to navigate the streets and get into position to pop up and take out that gun.

Sappy and Terry were taking out Charlies as the pilots maneuvered the choppers. Erickson and Brooks were doing the same. It wasn't easy hitting a running man as the drivers made sudden moves to keep from hitting a power line or another building.

"Seawolf, Seawolf. Kilo Rescue Three-zero-one. Do you copy?"

"Kilo Rescue Three-zero-one. Seawolf Two-six. We copy. Over."

"Seawolf. Kilo Rescue. When do you want us to come in? Over."

"Kilo Rescue. Seawolf Two-six. Will advise. Hold your position. Over."

With that, Bolton set up their run with Luscher. They'd be coming in at an angle to the golf course and the embassy. That way they wouldn't have to fly over the position where the big gun was.

The plan was to pop up to altitude just prior to making the strike and put two rockets on the .50s location—one rocket on the far building and one on the building behind the embassy. They'd use the door gunners on the break from the target to hit the building on the near side, then drop back down to low level, using the city for cover. As soon as Bolton would start shooting, the medevac—Kilo Rescue 301—would come in and land on the roof of the embassy building.

Once Kilo Rescue was down and started loading up the wounded, the Seawolf team would get set up for a second run from the opposite direction.

Bolton had finally worked the team into the correct position to start their gun run. He hit his mike button. "Kilo Rescue. Seawolf Two-six. You may start your descent. We are making our run, starting now! Do you copy?"

"Roger that, Seawolf. We are starting our descent to the embassy!"

The two gunships were dodging the tops of buildings as they accelerated toward their target. Just before Bolton got to the edge of the golf course, he pulled up on his collective, pulled back on the stick, and popped up to about 400 feet. Reaching the altitude goal, he nosed the chopper over so hard that all four crewmen felt almost weightless. He then lined his ship up with the suspected position of the heavy gun. Pulling the trigger twice, he sent two rockets into the trees lining the golf course. Pistol opened up with the flex guns, and the gunners cut loose with their barrage of .308s.

Before the first two rockets hit, Bolton was lining up on the far building. At the same time, he had his chopper gradually decreasing in altitude and gaining forward speed again.

On target, he punched off another rocket. The first two exploded on the golf course along with a shower of M-60 machine-gun fire.

The gunner on the right was concentrating his fire on the near embassy building. He could see the Australian medevac slowing as the chopper came in over the edge of the embassy rooftop.

Bolton lined up with the target in the back of the embassy and sent another rocket on its way. The far building ate up his other rocket as it exploded through the wall, sending debris skyward and to the street below.

That fourth rocket hit the other building as Bolton dropped his bird back down to the rooftops and exited the area.

Luscher had timed his hits perfectly. They had followed Bolton's to the letter. Terry notified Luscher that Kilo Rescue had made it safely to the landing pad on the top of the American embassy building.

As soon as Luscher broke off his run, Bolton started the team back around to hit her again from the opposite angle. It was another hair-raising experience dodging rooftops, power lines, and incoming fire from cross streets.

"Kilo Rescue Three-zero-one. Seawolf Two-six. I hope you're ready. We're fixing to start our second run. Do you copy? Over."

"Roger that, Seawolf. We have full load and are ready. On your mark! Over!"

"Roger that, Kilo Rescue. We are starting our run! Over!"

Zipping over the tops of the buildings, the Sea-wolves came screaming in on the enemy below. Popping up to 400 feet, Bolton squeezed off two rockets at the golf course. Then he sent one at each of the target buildings across the street from the embassy. Six of their M-60s barked out their tune, sending a shower of bullets down below.

The Australians pulled up into a hover and accelerated across the roof and up into the sky as Luscher was doing his thing with his small band of killers and rockets.

Bang, bang, bang, enemy bullets pierced the aircraft aluminum skin on Luscher's bird. It made a sound no one could forget. The crewmen prayed silently, hoping none of the VC rounds would find a critical spot within their helicopter that would send them to the streets below or crashing into the side of a building.

With the last rocket on its way, Luscher dropped down to three feet off the street and followed Bolton. Stout looked over the instruments to make sure all was well with the gunships' working parts. With no problem visible, they all breathed a little easier.

As Kilo One exited the area safely, he thanked the Seawolves for their help.

"No problem, Kilo Rescue. You guys take care," Bolton answered back.

Next was the other medevac. One problem, though—there were no more rockets left—and another two problems as well—there was a shortage of M-60 ammo and the fuel was also getting down there. Bolton advised the medevac that they should hold off trying to land at the embassy until the Seawolves could return with more rockets and machine-gun ammunition.

When it didn't seem things could get any worse, through the garbled communication on the radio it became clear that Digger One had been overrun and couldn't help out anymore.

There was one other place the choppers could go: the 9th Infantry base north of Saigon. It was actually closer. They also had helicopters at their location and could supply everything that was needed.

"Digger Two, Digger Two. Seawolf Two-six, do you copy? Over."

Another pause made their hearts skip a beat. God forbid this Army base was overrun also.

"Digger Two, Digger Two. Seawolf Two-six, Seawolf Two-six. Do you copy? Over."

"Seawolf, Seawolf. Digger Two. We copy. Over."

Thank God! "Digger Two. Seawolf Two-six. We need quick turnaround! Can you assist? Over."

"Roger that, Seawolf. We were kinda busy but we were expecting your call. Over."

"Roger, Digger Two. Our ETA three minutes. Over."

"Roger, Seawolf, we're ready for ya! Just come on in and set 'er down. We'll take it from there. Over."

They came on in, all right, into a disaster area. Just like Digger One, it had been hit bad. They saw chunks of twisted metal that used to be helicopter gunships, some in their revetments and some out on the runway, where they had probably been trying to get off the ground in a scramble.

The Army ground crew once again came through for the hungry Navy gunships under the worst possible conditions. The Seawolves were amazed at how well they performed under the circumstances. Sappy, Terry, Erickson, and Brooks didn't have to do a thing except load their door boxes. The Army guys took care of the copilots' flex guns, the rockets, and the JP-4 jet fuel.

This quick turnaround had to be a record breaker.

Again, when the choppers were in hover check the Navy crews popped a smart salute to their Army brothers. Luscher and the rest knew what faced the ground crew once the two gunships had departed. They'd have to go back to the job at hand, which was separating their friends from the blown-up helicopters scattered all over the runway.

This wasn't like going to the movies where combat was glamorous, he thought. Combat sucks!

Moments later the Seawolf team was approaching the airspace over the American embassy.

There to greet them was the circling Australian medevac. They were wisely orbiting at a much higher altitude, where ground fire couldn't reach them.

It didn't take long to get everyone in position to do the same thing they'd done for Kilo Rescue 301. This time they did it for Kilo Rescue 305.

On this attack, Bolton changed the order in which they ran their low-level runs. As usual, you never wanted to give Charlie a look at the same picture twice. That would almost guarantee that you'd get shot down.

25

Dodging in and out and around the tops of buildings to make a run on a .51 caliber machine gun was not the Seawolves' idea of fun, but it was one hell of a rush. The Australian medevac needed cover to get the rest of the wounded off the top of the American embassy building, and the Seawolves were their only hope of doing it safely.

Bolton cleared the last intersection that he used as a landmark to signal, then up they went, then over the top. He punched off two rockets and headed downhill toward the building on the far side of the embassy.

As the rockets impacted the trees on the golf course, he punched off another, sending it into the side of the target building, and then a fourth dart screamed toward the second building.

Both missles exploding on impact were followed by a rocket fired by Luscher. One after the other, along with a deluge of .308s, they kept the NVAs' heads down. That gave the medevac enough time to land on the top of the embassy building without incident.

As they loaded up the casualties, the Seawolf team made its way through, around, and over the Saigon city streets to reach the next point of their gun run. As they went, Sappy, Terry, Erickson, and Brooks were adding notches to their M-60s, dropping unsuspecting NVAs roaming the streets.

They'd been walking around and hadn't run into any opposition at all. And now the sun had come up and they could see well and their attention was suddenly drawn to the sound of helicopters approaching. No doubt they couldn't tell where it was coming from because of the echo off the surrounding buildings.

And then a helicopter gunship came flying around the corner, headed straight for them, no more than three feet off the ground, moving at 120 miles per hour. The rotor blades, turning so fast, made a weird screaming, popping sound as it turned sharply at the street intersection. The sound would have been so loud to those on the ground as to be deafening.

Imagine what the soldier on the ground would have seen. The chopper would have come at him at eye level. Hanging out the door was a man with his foot on top of a rocket pod, the other leg wrapped around a pole to keep him from falling out at the chopper's sudden movements. He wears tiger-striped fatigues, and his flight helmet—with the dark visor down, covering his eyes—makes him look like a one-eyed monster. He's pulling the trigger on his M-60 machine gun and the bullets are tearing up the street, rapidly walking toward you.

It would have been one Seawolf gunner the man would never forget—if he somehow managed to survive.

The two gunships maneuvering around and through the city streets kept the enemy baffled because the NVA couldn't figure out where they would be next.

"Kilo Rescue Three-one-five, Kilo Rescue Three-one-five. Seawolf Two-six, Seawolf Two-six. Do you copy? Over."

"Seawolf, Seawolf. Kilo Rescue Three-one-five. We copy. Over."

"Kilo Rescue Three-one-five. Seawolf Two-six. We are in position. Are you ready? Over."

"Seawolf. Kilo Rescue Three-one-five. We are a go. Over."

"Roger Three-one-five. On my mark." And with that, Bolton passed the point he'd been heading for and increased altitude.

"Three-one-five, Seawolf Two-six. *Mark!*" The first rocket was on its way to the suspected .51 caliber gun's location.

The Australian medevac lifted off the top of the American embassy building. The second rocket from Bolton's gunship blasted, then the third and the fourth, all right on target. Luscher's rockets came right in behind those and exploded too. Their gunners were shooting in all directions, trying to keep the NVAs' heads down or at least divert the enemy fire away from the departing medevac and toward the Seawolf gunships instead.

"Mayday! Mayday! Seawolf Two-six is going down!" Bolton yelled over the radio.

As he started his break, while Luscher was shooting under his belly, Seawolf 26 took one or more rounds in its jet engine from the .51 caliber. As they started to lose power, Bolton was able to pull her around and start his autorotation while he still had some altitude. Unfortunately, it didn't leave him a lot of options as to where to set it down safely.

So the chopper went down in the middle of the golf course.

Luscher had already launched his fourth rocket by the time Bolton had broadcast his Mayday. He continued his breakoff from the target and went down to low level. As he maneuvered his bird around the buildings and streets, working his way back to a point where he could cover his brothers on the ground, Sappy saw the Seawolf landing. "Two-six is down with a perfect autorotation, sir!" he said over the ICS.

"Roger that!" Luscher answered.

"Seawolf, Seawolf. Kilo Rescue Three-one-five. We are clear. I say again, we are clear."

"Roger that, Kilo Rescue, I copy!" Luscher answered.

"Two-four, Two-six! We're down in one piece but I don't know how long we'll stay that way! We're taking all kinds of fire!" Bolton said, panic in his voice.

"Roger that, Two-six! Keep your heads down! Here we come!" And with that, Luscher brought his bird up to altitude, nosed her over, and got ready to shoot. What he saw before him was not good at all.

Bolton was smack dab in the middle of the golf course, and NVAs were charging him from the far side treeline. It was the same treeline that had the heavy machine gun.

"Holy shit!" Luscher blurted out over the radio. The heavy machine gun had just opened up on them. Two of the biggest tracers he'd ever seen went blowing by his chopper.

Call it instinct, call it fear, call it nerves of steel or just plain dumb luck, Luscher popped off three rockets that went right back down the throat of the .51

caliber gun. Three high-explosive warheads put an end to it.

Terry and Sappy were dropping men by the bushel basket. So were Erickson and Brooks as they lay in a defensive position with their pilots next to their crippled bird. Their M-60s, and Pistol and Bolton shooting their M-16s, were killing tangos as fast as they came out of the treeline next to the golf course.

Luscher continued his run straight toward his teammates on the ground. "There's no fucking way you assholes are going to get your hands on my boys!" he shouted.

"You bet your ass!" Sappy added.

"Let's go get 'em!" Terry said.

"Let's do it!" Stout said.

Seawolf 24 brought his bird down toward Seawolf 26 and slowed to a hover, twenty feet above their friends. All six M-60s, white-hot from firing, were putting divots on the fairway, not to mention NVA bodies.

Luscher's bird was getting plugged full of holes as Bolton in Seawolf 26, over the little portable radio attached to the chest of his flight suit, told him to get out of there. Luscher's reply was to launch his last three rockets at almost point-blank range into the enemy as they charged out of the treeline. As the three thunderous explosions rocked Luscher's chopper, he maneuvered over down next to Bolton's and landed.

"They've got unexpended rockets on board, and we're empty!" Stout said over the ICS.

"Get 'em!" Luscher yelled.

He didn't have to say it twice. While all four gunners were laying down cover fire, Bolton, Pistol, and Stout pulled the six unused rockets out of the wounded bird and loaded them into Seawolf 24. Next was the extra arms and ammunition. Once that was done, everyone piled into the back.

Bolton plugged into Luscher's ICS and said, "We're ready! Now can you get us the fuck outta here?"

Luscher said, "No problem!" as he fired the rest of the rockets they had just loaded, all of which exploded way too close for comfort.

For a moment, Stout thought he saw body parts flying by his window.

Luscher slid the now very heavy chopper across the golf course and gradually up into the sky, all four gunners firing like crazy, two out each door.

Bolton pushed his ICS. "Luscher, you're one crazy son of a bitch!" he shouted.

"Thank you, sir," Luscher answered.

Once they reached a safe cruising altitude, Seawolf 24 pointed them toward their home base of Nha Be.

Bolton was thinking, That's enough of that shit.

Luscher was thinking, I can't wait to drop these guys off so we can get back to work.

26

Ever so gently, Luscher set his bird down at Nha Be. Bolton, Pistol, and their gunners got out and pulled their gear off the helicopter. Terry and Sappy, without a word spoken, started doing a quick turnaround. Stout got out of his copilot seat and checked the damage. They had taken a lot of hits, but nothing serious.

Bolton walked over to Luscher's door and had to yell over the sound of the jet engine and the whirling blades above their heads, "Where do you think you're going?"

"Back to work, boss!" Luscher yelled.

"Without a cover bird?" Bolton said.

"Are you kidding? I thought I saw a mamasan back there on the top of the embassy that had tits so big she could jump-start a 707! I gotta get a better look at that!" Luscher yelled, laughing.

With that, Sappy and Terry climbed back in their respective seats and cleared each side for hover check. Stout was strapped in and ready for takeoff. Luscher rolled on the power and started to pull up on the collective. The thin layer of dust on the ground began to blow away.

As Bolton backpedaled away from the lifting ship

he yelled, "You are certifiable, you crazy son of a bitch!"

Hover check complete and Bolton out of the way, Luscher started his bird down their short runway toward the river. As they gained speed they started gaining altitude. Out over the water they went and back up to battle speed.

Turning their gunship back toward Saigon, the four crewmen felt strange being alone in the sky with everyone on mother earth trying to shoot them down.

Once again the calls started flooding the airwaves for help. Among all the garbled talk, they heard something they all found troubling. Digger Two had been overrun and could no longer help with fuel or ammunition.

None of this was looking good. In the lone gunship the crew was wondering whether the U.S. was losing the war. Would they have a place to land when this was over? Or was this it? Were they going to have to fly out to sea and ditch in the ocean next to one of the Navy ships?

Luscher hit his ICS. "I know what you're thinking, boys!" he said. "Just remember, it ain't over till the fat lady sings!"

Terry hit his ICS. "Hey, if she's back here, I'm kickin' her ass out because we can't handle the extra weight!"

Dick hit his ICS. "When you do, make sure it's over some unsuspecting VC!"

They all had a laugh, then pressed on.

"Seawolf, Seawolf. Alpha Bravo One, Alpha Bravo One. Do you copy? Over."

"Alpha Bravo One. Seawolf Two-four. I copy. Over."

"Seawolf. Alpha Bravo One. We need assistance ASAP. What's your ETA? Over."

"Alpha Bravo One, ETA seven mikes. Over."

Alpha Bravo One was the Green Beret adviser at the President's Palace. Just like all the rest, they were being overrun. Luscher cranked her over as fast as she would go.

As they came upon the scene, they saw a large hole that had been blown in the front gate. A mass of NVAs was crowding through the hole and overrunning the inner courtyard. American troops were in plain sight on the top of the palace, shooting down into the crowd.

Luscher nosed the chopper over and went straight into attack mode. Sappy and Terry along with Dick were strafing the hell out of the inner courtyard. They could see chunks of concrete mixed with chunks of sod getting tossed back and forth across the courtyard along with bodies wrenching here and there as the .308s chewed up everything in sight.

Luscher lined up his sights and fired two high-explosive and two white phosphorus rockets. All four hit in the hole where most of the enemy were packed together.

The explosions might even have made the hole bigger, since chunks of concrete and the gate flew skyward, along with body parts.

By the time Luscher broke off his attack, Terry could see the NVA on the run. The four darts had done the trick. Even so, he and Sappy kept firing, taking men down.

"Way to go *Seawolf!* You guys are the greatest! Alpha Bravo One, out."

"Roger, Alpha Bravo One. You guys take care," Luscher answered.

On to the next call.

"Seawolf, Seawolf. Striker King, Striker King. We need assistance. Do you copy? Over."

"Striker King, Seawolf Two-four. Go ahead."

"Seawolf, Striker King. We've got 'em comin' over the wall. Can you assist? Over."

"Striker King, Seawolf Two-four. ETA eight mikes. Do you copy? Over."

"Seawolf, Striker King. We copy eight mikes. Over."

Another balls-to-the-wall flying time for Luscher and the crew. They were headed for a Green Beret outpost located just northwest of Saigon. Luscher had worked with them before, when he was flying training missions with the Army.

By this time the sun had climbed high in the sky. It was a clear day, and targets on the ground were just as visible as those in the air. As a result, Luscher decided he'd do this one up close and personal.

As he came in sight of the outpost and could see where everyone was, he dropped the bottom out and headed for the deck. Since he was familiar with this area, he lined up for a low-level rocket run.

"Striker King, Seawolf Two-four. You boys duck. I don't want to get ya with any ricochets. You copy?"

A familiar voice came back over the radio. It was Special Forces Sergeant David Gritzner. "Seawolf, Striker King. We know you! We copy!"

Terry and Sappy were each leaning way out of their doors, guns at the ready, feet on top of the rocket pods, braced for action.

Stout had his flex gun sight pulled down and his

eyes peeled. Luscher brought them in low and fast, dodging the tops of the taller trees and skimming the tops of the shorter ones, weaving in and out like a hungry wasp coming in for the kill.

Abruptly, they cleared the jungle and popped out into the open. The outpost lay before them, NVAs all over the walls and tangled in the wire.

Two spots had been blown open and Charlie was running through. Terry and Sappy were hitting those who were on the wall and hung in the wire. Stout opened up on the first hole they were coming up on. Luscher sent a white phosphorus rocket into the group going through the first hole, then punched off a second white phosphorus rocket into the second hole. The next rocket was high explosive, and it was placed on the wall, followed by another HE. The Seawolf chopper was hitting it so close, they were flying through debris that their explosions were tossing skyward.

Luscher's run took them in a half circle before he exited the area, also low and fast. He took them back into the jungle before circling around and popping back out, headed in the opposite direction.

One white phosphorus and two high-explosive rockets found their mark on the wall before the Seawolf gunship flew off again into the jungle.

Terry's and Sappy's M-60s found their mark across the outpost. Some of the Green Berets who were in hand-to-hand combat had their foes shot to pieces before their eyes. They were no doubt thankful for what had to be considered close air support.

Luscher took the chopper back up to 800 feet and orbited the area, letting the door gunners work out. It wasn't long before Striker King released them with a big thank-you; another satisfied customer.

As the lone gunship continued to orbit the now saved outpost, the radio communications became less scrambled. Clearly, things were starting to be brought under control. A slow wave of counterattacks against the NVA was catching up with the Seawolves' gunship efforts. The strikes had, by fortuitous accident, been placed in strategic spots that gave the MPs in their jeeps—with their .50 caliber machine guns—and the roving APCs a chance to recover, along with groups like the SEALs, who were fighting from building to building. Plus, some other air support had finally materialized from other locations.

Luscher got one last panicky call for help. It was from an ARVN outpost north of the Green Beret base they had just helped. A South Vietnamese lieutenant told them there was a large group of NVA retreating from their location. He wanted Luscher to keep them from getting away.

That sounded reasonable.

Away Luscher and the crew went, once again into the jaws of death. When they arrived, it was not a pretty sight.

The retreating NVA were already shot up, and were using women and children as cover so no one would shoot at them.

The lone Seawolf team circled like a vulture circles its prey. Meanwhile, the South Vietnamese lieutenant kept ordering the vulture to strike.

Sappy, Terry, Stout, and Luscher could all hear the demand. As they flew their circle, they regarded each other with a look of disgust. Since 0130 hours that morning, the four Seawolves had been working, and killing, for these same people who were now ordering them to kill innocent civilians. It seemed amazing, the disregard of human life the South Vietnamese officials had for their own people. Luscher told him to fuck off, and then they turned for home.

Their helicopter had so many holes shot in it that it would just barely fly by the time they got back to Nha Be.

It was like that all over the country. In fact, all the other Seawolf detachments had been through the same thing as Det. Two. The gunships in HAL-3 had taken so much damage that the entire squadron had to stand down for two weeks afterward because they had no helicopters that could fly.

Lieutenant Junior Grade John Luscher received the Silver Star and Distinguished Flying Cross for his choices that day. Saigon and South Vietnam had been saved. For what, many of the men had no idea.

Epilogue

It was a beautiful day in Saigon. Not a cloud in the sky, and just enough breeze blowing to keep the heat from being miserable.

Admiral Zumwalt was in the office of Admiral Veth, visiting in preparation for taking command of the naval forces in South Vietnam. As they stood there drinking an ice-cold Coke, Zumwalt's attention was drawn away from what Veth was saying and on to something else. That something else was out Admiral Veth's window. He turned and looked out his window to see what Zumwalt was staring at.

"Well, I'll be damned," Veth said. "He said that he'd do it, and by God he did just that."

Zumwalt asked, "Who said they would do what and did what?" as he kept staring out the window.

"When Spencer got here, he told me that if I would let him do what he wanted, he'd have our guys water-skiing behind PBRs on the Saigon River before he was done. And by God, he did just that!"

With that, both admirals stood there silently, staring out the window at a PBR going up the Saigon River, pulling a sailor behind it on water skis.

• • •

The combination of the nine detachments of Sea-wolves with the Sealords, Black Ponies, River Rats on the PBRs and Swift Boats, and the SEAL Teams had complete control over the Delta of South Vietnam and claimed victory. That took just four years. However, with the shift of policy that turned everything over to the South Vietnamese as the U.S. disengaged, the war was lost overnight.

It's a sad thing to make sacrifices and not be rewarded at the end. We still must remember that we made those choices. We made those sacrifices. Unfortunately, we weren't taught how to live with those choices and those sacrifices. So we are the ones who lose the sleep, have the nightmares, and suffer through the waking hours of regret.

We need to learn from our mistakes, meanwhile remembering that we can do everything correctly and still lose. That's life. That doesn't mean you quit. We must keep doing the best we can, and eventually it will come back around and it will be our turn to be rewarded. The only way we fail is if we stop trying.

For those who made the ultimate sacrifice—they're at the top of the hill of success in paradise, waiting for us to get there.

Index

INDEX

INDEX

INDEX

*Look for this extraordinary memoir of a man
who dedicated his life to everything
that is great and enduring about America. . . .*

A RANGER BORN

A Memoir of Combat and Valor
from Korea to Vietnam

by Col. Robert W. Black

Even as a boy growing up amid the green hills of rural Pennsylvania, Robert W. Black knew he was destined to become a Ranger. With their four hundred-year history of peerless courage and independence of spirit, Rangers are a uniquely American brand of soldier, one foot in the military, one in the wilderness– and that is what fired Black's imagination. In this searing, inspiring memoir, Black recounts how he devoted himself, body and soul, to his proud service as an elite U.S. Army Ranger in Korea and Vietnam– and what those years have taught him about himself, his country, and our future.

Now in hardcover from Ballantine Books
Available wherever books are sold.

*Don't miss these harrowing true combat
stories of Vietnam*

by Gary A. Linderer

PHANTOM WARRIORS
Book I

Here are some of the most courageous missions
executed by six-man LRRP, LRP, and Ranger teams
on their own deep behind enemy lines. These gripping accounts begin when the call first went out for
covert U.S. long-range reconnaissance patrols in
late 1965, continue through the battles of Tet, and go
all the way up to the final, tortured pullout. These
highly trained warriors were among the best
America had to offer, and they gave their best, no
matter how high the price.

PHANTOM WARRIORS
Book II

Phantom Warriors II presents heart-pounding, edge-
of-your-seat stories from individuals and teams.
These elite warriors relive sudden deadly firefights,
prolonged gun battles with large enemy forces,
desperate attempts to help fallen comrades, and the
sheer hell of bloody, no-quarter combat. The LRRP
accounts here are a testament to the courage, guts,
daring, and sacrifice of the men who willingly faced
death every day of their lives in Vietnam.

Published by Ballantine Books.
Available wherever books are sold.